Focus on Text

As schools shift to the Common Core, many English language arts teachers are left with questions about how their classrooms should look. *Is fiction out? Can I still do strategy instruction? Does close reading mean deliberating on each word?* Finally, there's a resource with all of these answers and more. In *Focus on Text*, bestselling author Amy Benjamin provides practical guidance on how to realistically implement the Common Core reading standards. Part I of the book examines misconceptions about the standards and what's really required. It also takes you inside classrooms to see how teachers are modifying their instruction. Part II tackles each reading standard for grades 4–8. You'll learn how to teach the standards with literary and informational texts and how to use them as a springboard for instruction in writing, language, speaking, and listening.

Topics include . . .

- Defining close reading and how it is different from word-by-word reading. When and how do students need to go over a text meticulously?
- How to use scaffolding through background knowledge to help students with challenging texts
- The best instructional practices to help students increase their range of reading and level of text complexity
- Ideas for teaching key concepts such as text structure, point of view, theme, stated and implied meanings, and the progression of ideas and characters
- Tweaking your assessments to better align with the Common Core—how to create reading check quizzes, unit tests, and cold reading tests to see if students are growing as readers
- And much, much more!

Throughout the book, you'll find teaching tips and practical resources to use with students, such as question starters and sentence stems. You'll also get a wide variety of classroom examples at different grade levels and with different texts. Whether you're experienced with the Common Core or just getting started, this book will give you exciting new ideas for making them work in your own classroom so your students grow as readers!

Amy Benjamin is a national education consultant and author of twelve books on teaching literacy. Before becoming a consultant, she was an award-winning English teacher in Montrose, New York.

Focus on Text

Tackling the Common Core Reading Standards, Grades 4–8

Amy Benjamin

Routledge
Taylor & Francis Group

NEW YORK AND LONDON

First published 2014
by Routledge
711 Third Avenue, New York, NY 10017

and by Routledge
2 Park Square, Milton Park, Abingdon, Oxon OX14 4RN

Routledge is an imprint of the Taylor & Francis Group, an informa business

© 2014 Taylor & Francis

Library of Congress Cataloging-in-Publication Data

Benjamin, Amy, 1951–
  Focus on text : tackling the common core reading standards, grades 4–8 / Amy Benjamin.
     pages cm
  Includes bibliographical references.
  1. Language arts (Elementary)—Curricula—United States.   2. Language arts (Elementary)—Standards—United States.   3. Language arts (Middle School)—Curricula—United States.   4. Language arts (Middle School)—Standards—United States.   I. Title.
  LB1576.B4377 2014
  372.6'044—dc23
  2013050052

ISBN: 978-0-415-73475-2 (hbk)
ISBN: 978-0-415-73343-4 (pbk)
ISBN: 978-1-315-81975-4 (ebk)

Typeset in Palatino
by Apex CoVantage, LLC

Contents

Acknowledgments

Eye On Education, with whom I began my career as an education writer and wrote eleven books, is now part of Routledge. With this change, I would like to thank the fine professionals at Eye On Education, notably founder and president, Robert N. Sickles. I am delighted to retain a relationship with my expert editor, Lauren Davis, now Acquisitions Editor at Routledge. I look forward to many future writing projects with Lauren and the staff at Routledge, as I expand my horizons to meet global needs for professional development in the field of education.

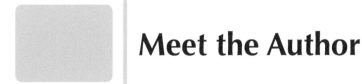

Meet the Author

After enjoying a long and rewarding career as an English teacher in the Hendrick Hudson School District in Montrose, New York, **Amy Benjamin** now works as a national consultant. Her goal is to improve education by helping teachers recognize the role that language plays in learning. As such, the Common Core State Standards, with their emphasis on literacy as a foundational skill across all subject areas, fit perfectly into her vision of education reform. Amy has been honored for excellence in teaching by Tufts University, Union College, and the New York State English Council. Her classroom was used as a model for standards-based teaching by the New York State Education Department. Amy lives in Dutchess County, New York, with her husband, Howard. Their son, Mitchell, lives in California and works in the television industry. This is the twelfth book that she has written for Eye On Education.

Introduction

This book is about classroom practices that use the Common Core Reading Standards as a foundation for the other Literacy Standards (Writing, Speaking and Listening, Language). In this book, you will explore the ten Reading Standards in grades 4–8, with a glimpse at the grades 3 and 9–10 grade bands to give you perspective.

Although the Common Core State Standards (CCSS) were adopted in 2010, implemented by 2013, and officially assessed by 2014 (give or take, depending on the individual states), many educators are still tentative about exactly what is expected in classrooms on a day-to-day basis. I have the privilege of working with teachers and their supervisors across the United States. I begin my workshops by asking them to express their familiarity with the Common Core (Literacy Standards only—I leave the math to someone else) on a scale of 1–5, with 1 being "never heard of it" to 5 being "know it thoroughly." I get a lot of 2's. By reading this book, I hope that you will come to consider yourself close to a 5, on the Reading Standards, at least, and that you will see how the other Literacy Standards blend into them.

As you know, the Common Core State Standards, aka Common Core Literacy Standards, are described in detail on their website, which is www.corestandards. org. The authors have been well-organized and thorough. The website is easy to navigate, but the information is voluminous, as it has to be. It's a lot to process. What follows is the original language of the Anchor Reading Standards, "thumbnailed" by my own simplified version in bold.[1]

So as not to overwhelm you with all thirty-two Literacy Standards, I've included the Writing, Speaking and Listening, and Language Standards in Appendix B.

Key Ideas and Details

1. **Read closely.** Read closely to determine what the text says explicitly and to make logical inferences from it; cite specific textual evidence when writing or speaking to support conclusions drawn from text.

2. **Track themes and summarize main ideas.** Determine central ideas or themes of a text and analyze their development, summarize the key supporting details and ideas.

3. **Understand and follow progressions.** Analyze how and why individuals, events, and ideas develop and interact over the course of a text.

Craft and Structure

4. **Know what the words and phrases mean in a given context.** Interpret words and phrases as they are used in a text, determining technical, connotative, and figurative meanings and analyze how specific word choices shape meaning or tone.

5. **Understand how and why the author has arranged the information according to certain organizing principles.** Analyze the structure of texts, including how specific sentences, paragraphs, and larger portions of text (e.g., section, chapter, scene, or stanza) relate to each other and the whole.

6. **Assess how point of view or purpose affects meaning.** Assess how point of view or purpose shapes the content and style of text.

Integration of Knowledge and Ideas

7. **Understand charts, graphs, and other numerical information and media in addition to just the words.** Integrate and evaluate content presented in diverse formats and media, including visually and quantitatively, as well as in words.

8. **Judge the validity of arguments.** Delineate and evaluate the arguments and specific claims in a text, including the validity of the reasoning as well as the relevance and sufficiency of the evidence.

9. **Compare texts that address similar subjects. Consider both content and style.** Analyze how two or more texts address similar themes or topics in order to build knowledge or compare the approaches the authors take.

Range of Reading and Level of Text Complexity

10. **Comprehend complex text.** Use exemplars in Appendix B of the Common Core Standards as a guide for grade level expectations (www.corestandards.org).

Regarding the range and content of the Reading Standards, the Core Standards document (www.corestandards.org) says:

> To become college and career ready, students must grapple with works of exceptional craft and thought whose range extends across genres, cultures, and centuries. Such works offer profound insights into the human condition and serve as models for students' own thinking and writing. Along with high-quality contemporary works, these texts should be chosen from among seminal U.S. documents, the classics of American literature and the timeless dramas of Shakespeare. Through wide and deep reading of literature and literary nonfiction of steadily increasing sophistication, students gain a reservoir of literary and cultural knowledge, references, and images; the ability to evaluate intricate arguments; and the capacity to surmount the challenge posed by complex texts.

This assertion strongly supports the use of canonical literature and traditional historical documents and texts of speeches that are widely considered to be touchstones of American culture. However, the studying of such texts should not preclude pleasure readings of choice by the students and their teachers. Without the element of readings-by-choice, students will not build up the necessary fluency, nor will they ever become life-long readers.

The CCSS can be crystallized as three essential instructional shifts:

1. Comprehending literary and nonfiction text at a level of complexity that increases as students go from grade to grade, until students are college and career ready at the time of graduation from high school;

2. Writing that draws from evidence synthesized from worthy text-based sources; and

3. Reading that strengthens comprehension skills and builds knowledge about language and the world.

To achieve these objectives, students need consistent growth in academic vocabulary. Vocabulary is acquired first receptively (listening and reading) and then productively (speech and writing). Tweeting and texting may be "speech written down," but academic writing requires control of formal conventions and the expected level of vocabulary. Students need to develop a range of levels of formality (language register) to function in various contexts. Students need to cultivate study skills that center on *careful, thorough reading of complex text.* To do this kind of reading and to answer questions and complete tasks based on it, students have to focus. The literacy demands of the Common Core, therefore, require a mode of thinking (i.e., concentration, as opposed to multi-tasking) that goes against the grain of the fast-paced, multi-tasking habits that most of us have developed in our everyday, device-driven lives. As much as the world has changed since we were in school (even if that was recently), the demands of college and (many) careers still require patience and depth of comprehension in reading.

I believe in the philosophy that durable learning happens through the process of solving problems. First, we frame the problem, then we enter it with some knowledge; we engage in a process of gathering more information, sifting through to see what we might need; then, through trial and error, communication, patience, and a positive attitude, we move toward a solution. What we've learned along the way—especially the skills we've learned, we get to keep. I'm not saying that we remember everything we read and comprehend at the time. What I'm saying is that we get to keep the skills and habits of conscientious reading if we continue to practice reading as a problem-solving process. The problem might be onerous, such as taking a test or interpreting the legalistic language of a contract; or it may be recreational, such as reading an interesting but difficult story.

This book is divided into two parts. Part One begins with the voices of teachers just like you who talk about how the Common Core is changing their classrooms. Part One then gives you general information about the Reading Standards, followed by a detailed definition of text complexity and readability measurements. We then attempt to rescue the babies from the bathwater of the Common Core, followed by a careful look at the relationship between instruction and assessment, because the Common Core does necessitate some tweaking of that relationship. Part Two tackles the Reading Standards one by one.

In the next section, we'll begin by looking inside classrooms at how the Common Core is being implemented.

Note

1. These are called "Anchor Standards" because they remain the same throughout grades 3–12, with specific competencies and increasing text complexity designated for each of the grade levels.

Part One

How the Reading Standards Are Being Implemented

Inside Classrooms

How Exactly Has the Common Core Been Changing America's Classrooms?

The Common Core State Standards have been described with words like "dramatic changes," "overhaul," "reform," "retool," and, "instructional shifts." So what exactly are educators saying about how the Common Core Literacy Standards, now in place for several years in most states, have actually changed their day-to-day classroom goals, plans, and actions?

In my work in education, I'm always most interested in what happens in classrooms. That is because I spent thirty-three years as a plain old teacher. I was always bemused by the difference between the educational schemes being hatched by state, district, and even building levels, that didn't affect me at all as a teacher. That means, accordingly, that any number of committees, task forces, flow charts, and strategic plans that occupied the higher-ups more often than not made no difference in how or what my students learned. "Education is cyclical. Education is trendy. Education is faddish. This too shall pass." We often hear these observations.

The Common Core State Standards are not radical. They build upon existing state standards. Let's say you have three school-aged children of your own. Your first-born is in the tenth grade, your middle child is in seventh grade, and your baby is in second grade. Are the children and teenagers themselves likely to notice significant differences in their education, compared to that of younger siblings? Well, the tenth grader might say to the seventh grader: "Hey, you guys are reading *A Long Walk to Water*? We read that in ninth grade." Your seventh grader might say to your second grader: "Whoa! These are your vocabulary words? These are hard. I don't even know some of these words." In other words, the changes that are most noticeable because of the Common Core are those that involve the ramping up of the complexity of whole-class texts and the emphasis on academic vocabulary.

> **Note**
>
> The Common Core State Standards are not a curriculum. The Standards
> are skills-based targets. A curriculum consists of specific content, as well as
> the targets for learning and assessments. Districts have the local control of the
> learning materials to be used to get students to where they need to be. Some
> districts allocate more control than others to individual teachers and depart-
> ments. Also, some states are what the textbook publishers call "adoption
> states," meaning that these states (famously California, Texas, and Florida)
> give their seal of approval to a limited number of textbooks from which
> the districts may choose. Therefore, the newest editions of textbooks reflect
> the Common Core, and educators draw their curriculum largely from these
> textbooks; but the Common Core itself does not constitute a curriculum.

The other changes, those that are indeed important but surely not dramatic, would be, and have been, noticed by teachers and administrators, if not so much by students themselves or parents. But the expectations of the Common Core do require pedagogical changes which have already been instituted, to varying degrees, in classrooms. I spoke to ten teachers at grade levels 4–8 about how the Common Core Literacy Standards change that pervades their teaching. "It doesn't have to be the most significant change. Just one difference that the Common Core Literacy Standards have brought about for you as a teacher that you think has affected how and what your students actually learn. And have altered your day-to-day classroom lives, not just a single lesson."

Grade 4

Amanda L. teaches in a suburban school with very high expectations. The community is notoriously well-heeled and well-educated, and the parents are highly knowledgeable and actively involved in their schools. Although Amanda's district maintains its "Number One in the County" status on the first round of Common Core-based state assessments, there was a significant drop in the grades of the students in grades 4–8, district-wide. The parents, citizens, and board of education are nervous about the drop in scores, fearful that they will lose their high status in the county if neighboring school districts start soaring ahead (and this district does not). Amanda has been teaching for about ten years.

Amanda says: "One of the biggest differences since the Common Core is that now I work with the students more on **paraphrasing and summarizing informational text**. Of course, everyone knows that the Common Core involves having students read more nonfiction, and, believe me, the District was fast to provide us with new books, great classroom magazines and online resources. But, in the past, we had our 90-minute reading block in the morning, where we used a workshop approach and leveled texts. Almost all of the writing was based on the children's own personal experience and opinion, with some book reports and creative writing. The science, math, and social studies did not involve writing. Now they do.

"And I don't ask them just to answer the end-of-the-chapter questions. All they did was to look at the questions and try to find the answers piecemeal in the text. They wouldn't read the whole thing. Now they have to, because I make them summarize what they read, either in writing or in their own words out loud in their groups. Each group has to work on a summary, and I tell them that I want to hear a lot of talking in the group as they are doing that. It's no problem asking fourth graders to talk. But they don't want to focus. I make them focus on what they read about.

"Paraphrasing is a big, big skill. I tell them: Turn the sentence inside out, which means to begin the sentence with a different word from the sentence you are paraphrasing. Decide which words you can't change and which ones you can. For example, if it's a sentence about biodiversity, they can't be trying to replace the word *biodiversity* with a synonym. Words in the glossary don't have synonyms, I tell them. But, let's say the sentence is something like, 'If you are looking for biodiversity, the co-existence of multiple life forms, you'll find it in a river,' I don't want them to change *biodiversity, river,* or *life forms.* But I want them to see that they can replace '*If you're looking for,*' with '*You can find . . .*' or something like that. Instead of multiple, they can say *many* or even numerous. Instead of co-existence, they can express the concept of many life forms *living together.* And it's more than just substituting one word for another. That's why I stress that they have to turn the sentence inside out. For a sentence like this one, they could maybe start with river (*Rivers are one place where you will find biodiversity*). And then, they need to practice sentence combining or sentence dividing: *Biodiversity means that many different life forms live together.* If you don't teach them that paraphrasing can also mean dividing one sentence into two, they will make a mess with all of the words. Dividing the sentences helps them control the main ideas. Keep it simple. That helps. But it's a skill that we practice at least three times a week.

"In science, social studies, and even math, I have them work in groups, with each group having to work together to write a paraphrase of the longest sentence in a paragraph. Then the groups read their work aloud to the class. That helps them learn the material, also, because each group is working on a different paragraph in the section of the chapter.

"And when we work on summarizing, I find it's extremely helpful to give the kids a shell, by that I mean a framework of sentence starters and transition words that will help them organize the information. These are simple frames, like: The section is called _____. It's about _____. It describes (or explains, or compares, or shows you how to . . ., etc.) _____.

"And then one more thing we do with the informational text, especially the science text, is that I have them decide what one question a paragraph is answering. Then, they write the question on a sticky note in the book and pass it to a partner. The partner has to read the paragraph and answer the question. It's can't be a yes/no question. This teaches them that every paragraph in informational text answers one main question. But it's hard to get them to understand the difference between a main idea question and a detail question. We work on that. It's hard, especially for some kids. When kids are having a hard time seeing the big picture, rather than a detail in a paragraph, I might make it more general: 'Look at your sub-heading. Turn it into a question.' It gets them to focus on the section as a whole."

Stephen G. teaches fourth grade in a district with a very mixed demographic. The school where Stephen teaches serves a community whose low socioeconomic levels, high number of non-native speakers of English and high mobility rates are markedly different from those of the other schools in the district. These conditions cause Stephen's school to have much lower test scores than those of other schools, and place his school under close scrutiny as well as an ever-changing carousel of "new programs" to raise scores.

Says Stephen, "The biggest change for us is that they don't want us to use leveled texts anymore. Well, I shouldn't say *anymore* like that. We can still use our classroom libraries for choice reading, and those are leveled texts, but we have to let the children choose any text they want. Instead of organizing the books by levels, now we organize them by topics. That has created some problems and it goes against what we have been told was right for a lot of years about matching kids to texts at their levels. It's getting used to a different philosophy about kids and reading, and, to be honest, some of us don't know if this is the right way.

"Now we have a science book that my students can't read by themselves. I'm not allowed to read aloud to them, except to get them started. So my science lessons have become much more of a reading lesson. I'm not saying that's bad, it's just that science used to be a lot more hands-on, and the kids were interested in it. Now, we don't have time for the labs. We still do some labs, but not nearly as much.

"Same with social studies. Our social studies time used to be very project-based, like the science. We had a lot of learning stations with geography games and jigsaw puzzles to learn the states, like that. We had crafts stations where kids would create flags for the different countries and do things like cave paintings and make vacation boxes to learn about different places in the world. The kids learned. We can still do those things, but we have less time for them because now the kids have to combine some kind of literacy activity with the projects. I make them write one complete sentence for their activity on an index card. And in their sentence they have to use a social studies vocabulary word from a list that I made for each station. To give you an example, they might be clipping images from the Internet to make a collage on a Power Point screen for a country, or a region, or a state, or a type of climate. Now they have to write a sentence that uses one word from the Academic Word List and another word from the Unit List. The Academic Word List would be all-purpose words like *specific, previous, purchase, obtain*. The Unit List has words just about the topic, like *arid, mountainous, coast, Great Lake*.

Grade 5

Elizabeth S. teaches fifth grade in a rural area in a Midwestern state. Some of the children of her school are in families of migrant farm workers, many of whom are undocumented residents.

"It's been hard to get used to giving students challenging text and doing whole class lessons because so many of my students don't speak English outside of school. I have to teach a lot more vocabulary, but we have a much better way of doing it than giving out word lists and filling in workbook pages. Most of my ELL's speak Spanish—not all of them, we have a lot of Mennonites here who speak German—but for the ones who speak Spanish—and I don't have much Spanish myself—the word components are very helpful. They're helpful for all of the children. Because of all the Latin that's in academic words—the prefixes and roots, I mean.

Elizabeth told me that she covers the walls of her classroom with visuals of the common Latin-based prefixes.

Tip

The Latin-based prefixes appear more regularly in informational text than in literary text. The prefixes that students should recognize in grades 1–3 are *re-, ex-, pre-, un-, dis-, non-, im-, mis-, mini-, maxi-*. The prefixes that they should recognize in the intermediate grades are *co- (con-, com-) syn- (sym-), in- (en-, inter-), sub- (sup-), e (ex-), a- (ab-)*, and the numerical prefixes *mono-, uni-, bi-, tri-, quad-, cent-, mil-)*.

"But you can't just give them a list of prefixes and say 'go learn these' and give a quiz. We have visuals around the room to refer to, and we do that all the time. We preview the articles and we look for words with the prefixes. The kids who know Spanish have an advantage because so many of these prefixes are found in everyday Spanish words. You'd be surprised how many English words they can figure out just from using their Spanish.

"In informational text at grade level, you'll find at least a half a dozen words that have these prefixes, but the prefixes don't always add understandable meaning to a word.

"For example, on a page, we might run into the word *replace* or *reclaim*, and that will be good because you can see how the prefix changes the meaning of the root word. But on that same page, we'll also run into *develop, important*, and *collect*. It's much harder to explain whether or not these words even have prefixes because they are not being added to an existing actual word. But even then, at least the children are trying to figure out a word based on a word-learning principle, and it gives us a chance to talk about how words really work. I still say it's better than the workbook with unrelated words approach, where the words are not grouped according to structure, and there's no context.

"We also have learning centers for the prefixes and roots. The other fifth grade teachers and I created word kits with laminated index cards in different colors for the prefixes and the roots. The children play with these, putting them together to form possible words. They do this in teams, to see how many words each team can put together. If a word is challenged, they have to show that it is in the dictionary. If not, that team loses. They're learning a lot of words that way, and being reminded again of the words that they do know. It's reinforcing."

Daniel R. teaches fifth grade in a well-known American city. This city has all of the problems, as well as the resources, of most such cities: considerable poverty, high mobility, disengagement from (and mistrust for) school, and large numbers of students with limited English proficiency. Daniel has made significant changes in the ways in which he accelerates academic vocabulary and academic language in general for all of his students, but particularly for the English language learners. "The kids here, the ones who do speak English at home, speak what you'd call a 'street' dialect. And when they write the way they speak—which they do—you see how steep the learning curve is.

"I have certain activities that seem to be improving their comprehension skills. I use pictures as a pre-reading activity. I'll show a picture that contains background knowledge about something they are about to read. I show it on the screen and we make a list of all the words and phrases that describe the pictures. We do this in what I'd call layers, like a think-pair-share. One thing I've been doing is having them work in groups with a small whiteboard. The first round is three minutes. Someone writes the words and phrases from the group on the whiteboard, then we pass to the next group and add. After three rounds one person—not the person who did the writing—will stand, show the whiteboard to another kid who reads it aloud. The other groups have to check off on their list what has already been mentioned.

"With the reading comprehension, we've been doing the paired reading, where one kid reads a sentence, or maybe a paragraph, and the partner has to summarize. Sometimes, I'll put a third kid in, and she has to answer three questions: *Do you agree with the summary? Are there any words you need to know more about? Can you add anything?*

"I'm working on getting them to pay special attention to cause-and-effect words, starting with *because.* I tell them: Whenever you see that word *because,* I want you to stop and think, because the word *because* answers a *why* question."

I asked Dan if he could think of anything he didn't do anymore that could be attributed to the Common Core. He smiled: "Well, we don't do round robin reading anymore," he said emphatically. "We're not allowed to do that. We get slammed for that. Probably a good thing. Nothing kills a page like round robin reading. It's painful. I don't know why I ever used to do it. Just a tradition, I guess.

"I've become much more conscious of generic academic words and I use them more than I would in natural conversation. I'm working on the habit of defining words as I use them. And using gestures. Also, when they say something halting, I'll rephrase it back to them. I do that a lot. I've had to become a lot more aware that so many of my words are new to not only the ELL's, but to these other kids as well. By teaching to the ELL's, everybody benefits, really."

Grade 6

Kyle M. is principal of a 6–8 middle school in a small suburban district that is closely associated with a cluster of surrounding districts that are also small but that have a higher socioeconomic demographic. Consequently, the community has a habit of comparing Kyle's school negatively with the surrounding districts. ("*Why can't we be like the _____ schools?*") So as you can imagine, there is a great deal of emphasis placed on test scores that are made public.

"I'm not going to get into a whole competitive thing about the test scores," Kyle says. "I don't think chasing the numbers is the way to go. The kids come to us from two K–5 schools that both use leveled texts in a workshop literacy block. So when they get here, most of them are within two grade levels on their reading, but I have to say that the biggest complaint I get from the teachers is about the writing. 'These kids can't write!' They write using texting abbreviations, and that drives the teachers crazy.

"We've been doing a lot of work on paraphrasing the informational text. I want the sixth grade teachers to have the students writing at least one paraphrase of a paragraph every week. I really think they should be doing that every single day, but once a week has been enough of a battle. The teachers complain about having to correct all the writing. I think some of them are not that comfortable correcting for the grammar, but that's another story.

"I think we need work on writing complete sentences that have meat on the bones. The kids are used to writing stories, poems, personal experience, that type of thing. But the paraphrasing is what they need. It gets them focused on academic vocabulary and writing sentences that don't just repeat the question, like they do when they're answering end-of-chapter questions. I'd like to see sentences that don't just parrot the words in the question and then end with not much information."

Grades 7 and 8

"People say the Common Core doesn't make much difference to them. They think it's the same thing we've always done with a different label. But for me there's definitely a difference in the assessments and, working backwards from that, there's a big difference in what I emphasize in my teaching about literature." So says Lynda, who teaches seventh and eighth grade English language arts.

"I have a lot of test questions and ready-made tests on the whole-class literature on file. I'm in the process of slowly revisiting all of them to align to the Reading Standards. It's a lot of work, but I know that if I don't do that, there will be gaps in the kinds of questions the kids have to answer on the tests that the state gives. I can't just do that kind of overhaul in one year. But even starting to do it has made me aware of the kinds of questions—the kinds of Standards— that I haven't addressed.

"But the biggest difference in the assessments that I give as a unit test—the thing I never did before in my twenty-plus years of teaching, is the cold reading. If I taught a story, I tested what I had taught on that story. It was all very self-contained: You're in my class. You read the story. We learned more about the story in class. We maybe did a literature circle, some graphic organizers, took notes off the board, had a vocabulary list, maybe did a little outside research about the setting of the story or the author. Then, we had a test that reflected that. Now, and this is the big difference, I feel I have to include some kind of reading comprehension passage that is just as challenging, maybe something else by the same author or from the same time period or about the same topic. Then they get questions that are aligned to the Standards 1–6. That's what I mean by a cold reading. And I tell them which Standards align to which question, and they keep track and I keep track of the Standards we need more work on. It sounds like a lot of work, but if I ask three questions for three different Standards, it's not that bad. I hope it's helping. But that's it: including that cold reading and the questions that match those Standards."

So the Common Core does not reside in some three-ring-binder that only the curriculum coordinator reads. Nor does it radicalize what we've always done. I see it as an enrichment, a refinement, and an accountability system for infusing high level thinking that is expressed through written and spoken language.

2 Text Complexity and Readability Measurements

According to the Common Core, it is not enough for students to simply "know how to read" if, by that, we mean that they can decode, even with fluency. (Fluency is the ability to read aloud at the pace of ordinary speech, to animate the text with appropriate expression, and to make no or very few mistakes in decoding words.) Fluency, though necessary for comprehension, is not to be confused with comprehension itself. Sometimes, comprehension is achieved only through painstaking rereading, where the reader makes frequent meaning-making stops—a process that can hardly be called fluent but that results in comprehension of dense and difficult text. Think of comprehension as swimming from one side of the pool to the other without assistance. Think of fluency as swimming through clear water. The kind of reading we're talking about in this book is more like slogging through a swamp: You have to move slowly, conscious of obstacles. You have to anticipate what might lurk around you. You might need special equipment. You certainly need plenty of time and an attitude that respects complex text as demanding effort.

Now picture a gym. Go over to the free weights. They are all the same shape and color. They are made of the same material. Pick one up from the left side of the rack. Do some reps. Be careful to use the proper form. Now look further down the rack and pick up another free weight. Using the same form that you used for the lighter weight, you'll probably find that you can do fewer reps. The variable is the weight: more weight, fewer reps.

That is the concept of text complexity and the Reading Standards. The Standards remain the same throughout the grade levels (3–12). (The primary grades include foundational concepts of decoding and fluency.) The variable is the complexity—the level of difficulty—of the texts that students are expected to handle. With reading, as with strength training, success depends not only on practicing, but on the right kind of practicing. The right kind of reading practice for college and career readiness incorporates all of the Reading Standards. Although the Reading Standards are overlapping and interlocking, we need to focus on particular ones, depending on the texts we are reading. Just as, at the gym, you do exercises that focus on particular muscle groups, when your form is right, your biceps and triceps are not on vacation when you are working on your pecs.

So how do we judge text complexity? The Common Core provides a model for three dimensions of text complexity:

1. **Quantitative measures**
2. **Qualitative judgments**
3. **Background of the reader; task to be done with the reading materials**

Quantitative measures used to be the only way to measure the "difficulty" of a text, usually calibrated as "grade levels." Several brands of quantitative measurement formulas are well-known. Some are simply metrics based on the average number of words in a sentence and the number of multi-syllabic words in a passage. Others take finer considerations such as the number of times given words are repeated in the text because the presence of repeated words in a text probably makes it more accessible. Some formulas even account for the kinds of word that join clauses: compound sentences are generally easier to process than complex sentences or sentences having a lot of relative pronouns. The problem with quantitative measures is that they are designed to judge the difficulty of reading material without ever actually reading it. That is how we get a book like *The Grapes of Wrath* to appear to be on a second grade level.

The Common Core adds **qualitative measures** to judge text complexity. Qualitative measures consider subjective qualities such as whether the text is organized in a non-linear manner (going back and forth in time, having multiple narrators, interposing narrative content with philosophical content, etc.); the commonness (not just the length) of the words and the familiarity of the style of language; the expectations that the author had of the reader's understanding of the topic; and whether there are multiple levels of meaning and/or irony.

The third dimension of text complexity, "reader and task," reinforces the **background knowledge of the reader** and adds the consideration of what the reader is expected to do with the text. Is the reader expected to answer a few literal-level questions? Write a summary? Analyze it? Synthesize it with other information? Evaluate it? Paraphrase?

Let's squash a misunderstanding about text complexity: For the most part, determinations of text complexity are objective. Teachers who look at a text and then conclude, "Well, this text would be considered complex for Jack but not for Jill," are probably missing the point: Our judgments about text complexity should be based *primarily* on the objective criteria (quantitative and qualitative). If you look at the outline in Figure 2.1, you will see that considerations that take individual readers into account do appear twice, once under "Qualitative measures" as "knowledge demands" (II, C), and then again under "Reader and task" (III, A).

How the Common Core Evaluates Text Complexity

I. Quantitative measures
   A. Average length of sentences
   B. Average number of words in sentences

II. Qualitative measures
   A. Complex structure (non-linear time order, multiple narrators, stream of consciousness, multiple settings, complicated graphic information that has to be integrated with the text)
   B. Language conventionality and clarity (language that simulates dialect, heavy use of technical terminology, stylized language, poetry)
   C. Knowledge demands (amount of background knowledge that the author expects the reader to have)
   D. Levels of meaning (subtleties created through symbolism, allusion, figurative language, implications)

III. Reader and task
   A. Background knowledge of the reader, relative to this text
   B. Sophistication of thinking required by the task that you are asking the students to do regarding this text: Where does the task lie in the continuum of low-to-high level thinking skills?

Figure 2.1

However, when we examine a text under the lens of the Common Core's definition of text complexity, we should be thinking about objective characteristics of the text first and foremost, with particular reader considerations taking a secondary place. This may well be a paradigm shift in the way we match text to students. Think of text complexity as the height of a standard basketball hoop. Rather than lowering the hoop, we teach aspiring players the skills necessary to reach it.

To give you an idea, the literary and information passages that follow are considered appropriate for the Grade 4–5 band (www.corestandards.org).

Literary Text Sample for Grades 4–5

Natalie Babbit, *Tuck Everlasting* (1975).

The sky was a ragged blaze of red and pink and orange, and its double trembled on the surface of the pond like color spilled from a paint box. The sun was dropping fast now, a soft red sliding egg yolk, and already to the east there was a darkening to purple. Winnie, newly brave with her thoughts of being rescued, climbed boldly to the rowboat. The hard heels of her buttoned boots made a hollow banging sound against the boards, loud in the warm and breathless quiet. Across the pond a bullfrog spoke a deep note of warning. Tuck climbed in too, pushing off and settling the oars on to their locks, dipped them into the silty bottom in one strong pull. The rowboat slipped from the bank, then, silently, and glided out, tall water grasses whispering away from its sides, releasing it.

Here and there the still surface of the water dimpled, and bright wings spread noiselessly and vanished. "Feeding time," said Tuck softly. And Winnie, looking down, saw hosts of tiny insects skittering and skating on the surface. "Best time of all for fishing," he said, "when they come up to feed."

He dragged on the oars. The rowboat slowed and began to drift gently toward the farthest end of the pond. It was so quiet that Winnie almost jumped when the bullfrog spoke again. And then, from the tall pines and birches that winged the pond, a wood thrush caroled. The silver notes were pure and clear and lovely.

"Know what this is, all around us, Winnie?" said Tuck, his voice low. "Life. Moving, growing, changing, never the same two minutes together. This water, you look out at it every morning, and it looks the same, but it ain't. All night long it's been moving, coming in through the stream back there to the west, slipping out through the stream down east here, always quiet, always new, moving on. You can't hardly see the current, can you? And sometimes the wind makes it look like it's going the other way. But it's always there, the water's always moving on, and someday, after a long while, it comes to the ocean.

Task: Students read Natalie Babbit's *Tuck Everlasting* and describe in depth the idyllic setting of the story, drawing on specific details in the text, from the color of the sky to the sounds of the pond, to describe the scene.

Informational Text Sample for Grades 4–5

Melvin Berger, *Discovering Mars: The Amazing Story of the Red Planet* (1995).

Mars is very cold and very dry. Scattered across the surface are many giant volcanoes. Lava covers much of the land.

In Mars's northern half, or hemisphere, is a huge raised area. It is about 2,500 miles wide. Astronomers call this the Great Tharsis Bridge.

There are four mammoth volcanoes on the Great Tharsis Bridge. The larger one is Mount Olympus, or Olympus Mons. It is the biggest mountain on Mars. Some think it may be the largest mountain in the entire solar system.

Mount Olympus is 15 miles high. At its peak is a 50 mile-wide basin. Its base is 375 miles across. That's nearly as big as the state of Texas.

Mauna Loa, in Hawaii, is the largest volcano on earth. Yet, compared to Mount Olympus, Mauna Loa looks like a little hill. The Hawaiian volcano is only 5 miles high. Its base, on the bottom of the Pacific Ocean, is just 124 miles wide.

Each of the three other volcanoes in the Great Tharsis Bridge are over 10 miles high. They are named Arsia Mons, Pavonis Mons, and Ascreas Mons.

(NASA's Informational sheet on Mars: www.nasa.gov/worldbook/mars/mars_worldbook.html)

Task: Students explain how Melvin Berger uses reasons and evidence in his book *Discovering Mars: The Amazing Story of the Red Planet* to support particular points regarding the topology of the planet.

And here are literary and informational samples considered appropriate for the Grade 6–8 band.

Literary Text Sample for Grades 6–8

Susan Cooper, *The Dark is Rising* (1973).

He was woken by music. It beckoned him, lilting and insistent. Delicate music, played by delicate instruments that he could not identify, one with rippling, bell-like phrase running through it in a gold thread of delight. There was in this music so much of the deepest enchantment of all his dreams and imaginings that he woke smiling in pure happiness at the sound. In the moment of his waking, it began to fade, beckoning as it went, and then he opened his eyes as it was gone. He had only the memory of that one rippling phrase as it still echoed in his head, and itself fading so fast that he sat abruptly in bed and reached his arm out to the air, as if he could bring it back.

The room was very still, and there was no music, and yet Will knew that it had not been a dream.

He was in the twins' room still; he could hear Robin's breathing, slow and deep from the other bed. Cold light glimmered around the edge of the curtains, but no one was stirring anywhere; it was very early. Will pulled on his rumpled clothes from the day before, and slipped out of the room. He crossed the landing to the central window, and looked down.

Task: Students explain how the author uses visual imagery to explain the effects of music, giving several specific examples from the text.

Informational Text Sample for Grades 6–8

John Steinbeck, *Travels with Charley: In Search of America* (1997, 1962).

I soon discovered that if a wayfaring stranger wishes to eavesdrop on a local population the places for him to slip in and hold his peace are bars and churches. But some New England towns don't have bars, and church is only on Sunday. A good alternative is the roadside restaurant where men gather for breakfast before going to work or going hunting. To find these places inhabited one must get up very early. And there is a drawback even to this. Early-rising men not only do not talk much to strangers, they barely talk to one another. Breakfast conversation is limited to a series of laconic grunts. The natural New England taciturnity reaches its glorious perfection at breakfast.

I am not normally a breakfast eater, but here I had to be or I wouldn't see anybody unless I stopped for gas. At the first lighted roadside restaurant I pulled in and took my seat at a counter. The customers were folded over their coffee cups like ferns. A normal conversation is as follows:

WAITRESS: "Same?"
CUSTOMER: "Yep."
WAITRESS: "Cold enough for you?"
CUSTOMER: "Yep."
(10 minutes)
WAITRESS: "Refill?"
CUSTOMER: "Yep."
This is a really talkative customer.

Task: Students determine the figurative and connotative meanings of words such as *wayfaring, laconic,* and *taciturnity,* as well as phrases such as *hold his peace* in John Steinbeck's *Travels with Charley.* They analyze how Steinbeck's specific word choices and diction impact the meaning and tone in his writing and the characterization of the individuals and places he describes.

"But my students can't read this! This text is way above their comprehension level! They can't understand these tasks!" is what you are probably saying. You're right, in a way. Without intervention, without scaffolding, without a great deal of practice, your students probably cannot read the complex text that the Common Core requires and do the tasks that meet the Writing Standards.

Acquiring those skills is a major reason why children and teenagers come to school.

> **Note**
>
> This is not to say that students shouldn't have ample opportunities to read text that is easy and interesting. Without leisure reading, students will simply not be getting enough knowledge about language and the world to build the necessary background.

On Babies and Bathwater

3

Correcting Misunderstandings about the Common Core

Like mushrooms after a rainstorm, myths about the Common Core flourish and reappear insistently. Most of these myths amount to exaggerations of the instructional shifts, and these exaggerations result from the tendency to oversimplify. Let's clean house.

Bathwater: Because of the Common Core, there is to be very little traditional literature, such as poetry, stories, and drama. It's all about nonfiction now.

Baby: The Common Core recommends a 50%–50% ratio of literary and informational text on the elementary level, gradually tipping that balance to 70% of informational text by the time students are in grades 9–12. However, the 70% of informational text includes the *entire* school day, not just English class. When you consider that most of what is read in subjects other than English class is informational, you realize that English teachers are *not* expected to jettison half of their novels, poetry, and plays. All the English teachers need to do to make things balance out is to include a bit more informational text, and that informational text can (and should) be related to the literature already in place. English teachers may have to let go of a novel or two—or, teach only the highlights of some of the longer works.

Myth: Memoirs, biographies, and autobiographies count as nonfiction. We do that, so we don't have to change anything to meet the Common Core requirements.

Baby: Well, not really. While it is true that stories of real lives in real places are nonfiction, they are written in a narrative-type structure and with literary-type language. If you look at the text samples on the Common Core website in Appendix B, you'll find that most of the samples of informational text do not have that literary style.

Rather, they are primary source documents from history (Supreme Court decisions, great speeches, excerpts from the United States Constitution); essays about social issues arguing a point of view; scientific and technical reports that often use charts and graphs in addition to paragraphs. The Common Core requires that students amass substantial experience in a true range of text types and purposes for reading. While we can certainly continue to give students those wonderful choices of memoir and life stories, we can't in good conscience check off "done" in the informational text column just on that basis alone.

Bathwater:	The Common Core really doesn't require very much change.
Baby:	The amount of instructional shifting you and your school need to do depends on how much you have already been teaching in a way that develops (not just expects—not just assesses) literacy skills as a means to learn about the world. Educators who have already been making decisions based on formative assessments and backward design (teaching towards known competencies) may be able to transition easily into the Common Core. On the other hand, if your school looks the way it might have looked in the 1960s or before—with the teacher dispensing knowledge like worms to a nest full of hungry baby birds—then Common Core teaching will be much more student-centered and skills-driven than the work you've done until now. Disappointed in your school's scores on the new Common Core assessments? That's your barometer as to the extent to which you and your colleagues need to change.
Bathwater:	The assessments for the Common Core are (will be) unfair.
Baby:	The Common Core assessments for literacy—whether they are created by SBAC (Smarter Balanced Assessment Consortium), PARCC (Partnership for Readiness for College and Careers), or by your state education department—will emanate from the Reading and Writing Standards, and blended into those, the Language Standards. You will not be able to "worksheet" or "test prep" your way into these assessments because you cannot predict the content of the reading passages. You can only give students routine practice—not for the test—but for improving their skills as readers. The more they read, the more background knowledge they will amass, the more vocabulary they will know, the more word groups they will be able to chunk, the faster they will be able to make sense of text at increasingly complex levels. The more genres they read,

20

the better they will be able to write in those genres. And the more you share the Reading Standards with them and show them how your comprehension questions align to them, the better they will become at handling the types of questions they will encounter on the Common Core assessments. The assessments will be challenging and reflective of the Standards, particularly the Reading Standards. I'm going right out on that limb here and asserting that the assessments will not be unfair if your instruction has been aligned to the Literacy Standards, even the ones (Speaking and Listening) that are not (directly) assessed.

Bathwater: The Common Core is another passing fad in education.

Baby: Given the vast amount of funding, publicity, and preparation—not to mention the underlying need to have more rigor in literacy and math in American schools—it is highly unlikely that the Common Core is "another educational fad." I know that education is notorious for being faddish, that we're often saying "Oh, _____ is really just like _____ with another name." Granted, trends come and go, and we are often renaming things. I write this in my fortieth year as an educator, not counting the sixteen—eighteen, if you count nursery school.

When I first began my teaching career in the 1970s, students chose their tracks, broadly based upon whether or not they intended to continue their academic education after high school. In those classes where students were not choosing to take the New York State English Regents Exam ("the Regents," as it is known), there were no standards. There was a highly localized (classroom to classroom) curriculum, and even though we were supposed to hand in planbooks—for tenured teachers, monthly—no one scrutinized them for rigor. If the students were not making a ruckus, if they were allowed to walk across the stage to pick up their diplomas on Graduation Day, no one asked any questions.

Then along came the mid-1980s, and in response to that infamous *Nation at Risk* report condemning American education in the strongest language possible, something came along in New York called the "Regents Action Plan." It required that all students pass "Regents Competency Tests." This involved composing a business letter, usually regarding a defective or undelivered product, assembling a report from a list of data, and writing a persuasive essay about a topic requiring no outside information or facts, just the student's opinion on school uniforms, cafeteria offerings, or video games in the student lounge. It seems laughable now, but at the time, the RCT, as they came to be called, constituted a major threat to the status quo. Rife were the predictions that students would "drop out in droves" rather than have to pass it.

The late 1990s brought shocking news: the English Regents Exam was no longer optional for all but the most disabled students. It would be a 6-hour test, given over 2 days, requiring four substantial essays. I was not alone in believing that it would never happen, or, if it did, that it would happen once only.

My point in all the ancient history is that, as a whole, we really have not lowered standards *once they are put in place*. We have risen to challenges in the last two "great waves" that I described. Yes, there is push-back on the Common Core. There are parents and parent organizations who keep their children home on the day of the tests. Three states at this writing—Virginia, Minnesota, and Nebraska—have opted out, joining the original holdouts, Texas and Alaska. A few more states may join them as naysayers to the Common Core. But, whether they are Common Core states or not, I doubt if they are going to hold their students to a lesser standard than the vast majority of states who remain committed to the Common Core, along with its testing.

Bathwater: Because of the Common Core, teachers are not allowed to give any pre-reading information. We just have to throw text at students and have them sink or swim.

Baby: The Common Core Reading Standards culminate in having students understand complex text that they read independently (Reading Standard 10). Pre-reading explanations should not be eliminated altogether, but they should be pared down from the extensive work on "connections" that many teachers have been doing. The idea is to maintain the integrity of the challenges inherent in the text. In our zeal to have students understand the content of the text, rather than to work through it, we may have eliminated the need for well-honed reading skills.

When we say that we should not be "spoon-feeding" students, that does not mean that we don't give them any utensils to eat with at all, or that we don't model how to eat with a spoon, or that we don't even open the jar for them. There will never be a "just right" formula for how much pre-reading explanation we should give. That will depend on the text, the students, and the task. It remains a good idea to spend a little time contextualizing what students are given to read (text-to-world connections) and arousing their interest (text-to-self connections). There is no harm in helping students meet a work of literature by pointing out its similarities in content, language, style, and structure to familiar works. To achieve the "just right" balance, we need to keep in mind that we are not just teaching content: We are teaching to one or more Reading Standards, using the reading material to build knowledge and skills, not just knowledge.

Pre-reading instruction is best when it launches a successful (and challenging) reading experience and can be a touchstone as the reading progresses.

A pre-reading activity that I always liked preceded the reading of *To Kill a Mockingbird*. When the students entered class, they would find their desks covered with spread-out newspaper pages, and there would be crayons within reach. I asked them to draw a picture of the street where they lived when they were six years old, including their various neighbors, and the route that they took to walk to school or the bus stop. Then, I would ask for volunteers to explain their drawings to the class. I found that being able to hold the newspaper in front of them and explain something familiar and interesting to them relieved their anxiety in public speaking. (And, the explanation was *voluntary*.) This was a good language-building activity and a good launch into *To Kill a Mockingbird*, which begins with a detailed description of a neighborhood. Most novels begin with a detailed description of a place, a place that readers have to mentally construct. Novice readers tend to be impatient with lengthy descriptions. My "draw your neighborhood" activity was worthwhile because it connected students to key themes of *To Kill a Mockingbird*, the themes of community, childhood memories, and childhood perspectives. We were able to revisit that experience and use its vocabulary (*perspective, community, tradition, ostracism*) at various points in the novel. Now, it needs to be said that the point of the "draw your neighborhood" experience is not to turn English class into art class. We are not creating masterpieces. That is the message sent by the newspaper and crayons, as opposed to paper and pencil, which would have felt less childlike. I wanted the students to feel like younger children as they drew expansively and with crayons so that they could relate to the point of view of Harper Lee, who wrote about her childhood with the voice and perspective of an adult (Reading Standard 6).

The "draw your neighborhood" activity connects students to *To Kill a Mockingbird* but certainly does not obviate the need to read it. Good pre-reading activities are springboards as well as touchstones.

The extent to which teachers should front-load reading experiences will always be controversial. I disagree with the chief authors of the Common Core Literacy Standards David Coleman and Sue Pimentel when they assert that cold readings are the way of the real world. In my world, except when I take a reading comprehension test (which is never), I do have background information and connections before I read something. Only in the world of *testing* is one expected to execute timed, close readings of random passages, unpredictable and unrelated to each other, while having no background or purpose except to answer multiple choice questions or write an essay that only an evaluator will read.

When I read for professional purposes, I read books or journals. I don't order random books. I order books because I know something about them; I have expectations. Books themselves usually have various features that prepare the reader: titles, sub-titles, tables of contents, introductions, chapter titles, and introductory paragraphs that set up expectations within the titles. If I don't understand something in a book, and I think it is important to my purpose for reading, I stop reading and get information, usually by googling it.

As for journals, don't most journal articles begin with an abstract? I have never thought: "I will not read this abstract because it will rob me of the pleasure of making my own meaning out of this journal article on the neuroscientific findings about how mildly dyslexic pre-adolescents process affixes." I read abstracts for two reasons: 1) to determine if the journal has information that I need, and 2) to make it easier to understand the technical information that I am about to read.

When I read for business purposes, such as reading contracts, I certainly have a context, background information, and a purpose for reading. I don't have to read it in a hurry. I can ask for clarification from a nearby human.

When I read for leisure purposes, I always have context and background. What is a book review? A recommendation from a fellow reader? An advertisement?

So, if we need to train students to do cold reads, let's do that as a run-up to the test. Students will be better able to handle cold reads if they build their reading muscles through authentic and supportive reading contexts. That is not to say that they don't need test prep a few weeks prior to the test. But, and we can't emphasize this enough, let's not confuse test prep with education that draws from and prepares students for authentic reading situations for college, careers, business, or leisure.

Bathwater: Don't teach reading strategies anymore.

Baby: In *7 Keys to Comprehension* (2003), Susan Zimmerman and Chryse Hutchins delineate seven reading comprehension strategies that they believe can and should be explicitly taught through modeling, practice, and assessment: 1) create mental images; 2) use background knowledge; 3) ask questions; 4) make inferences; 5) determine the most important ideas or themes; 6) synthesize information; and 7) use fix-up strategies. In *When Kids Can't Read: What Teachers Can Do* (2003), Kylene Beers recommends explicit teaching of a different set of strategies: Clarifying, comparing and contrasting, connecting to prior experiences, inferencing (including generalizing and drawing conclusions), predicting, questioning the text, recognizing the author's purpose, seeing causal relationships, summarizing, and visualizing. Says Beers: "While teachers almost always agree that the strategies … are important, they often resist teaching them directly; instead, they hope that awareness of and competency with these strategies are the by-products of class discussions. However, if we really want to affect students' comprehension abilities—as opposed to affecting their understanding of one particular text—then we must realize that for at least some of our struggling readers, we need to teach comprehension strategies explicitly and directly" (p. 44–47).

So, why has the myth developed that teaching reading comprehension strategies goes against the Common Core? And, if it is beneficial to learn the strategies, how does learning them improve comprehension in authentic reading situations (as opposed to answering test questions). The "baby" here is that some students, especially struggling readers, may need to learn how to apply the strategies. The "bathwater" is thinking of the strategies as ends in themselves, or in "applying" the strategies to easy text, that is, text that the reader could have easily understood without having to say things like "I activated my background knowledge" or "I predicted." Arguably, the strategies named above are results, not causes, of habitual reading. There is a strong, if obvious, relationship between those who read habitually (and voluntarily) and those who read competently. Reading strategies do not comprise curriculum: It is the reading itself, along with rich social experiences and text-based writing, that creates the literacy-building part of curriculum. In their research published in *Language Arts* (2013), Beth Maloch and Randy Bomer report on the efficacy of explicit strategy instruction on comprehension. They conclude that such instruction is effective *if* it is embedded within a larger pedagogy for reading informational texts. This larger pedagogy must rely heavily on engaging students in a wide range of reading material that will interest them, and creating an environment where reading is social, interactive, recursive, varied, and viewed as a positive, if challenging, experience.

The set of reading strategies listed above are helpful if used properly, harmful or useless if imposed upon students unnecessarily. (I say that they can actually be harmful because, if imposed on readers unnecessarily, having to use the strategies can interfere with a reader's concentration, not to mention a reader's interest and involvement in the text.) In the primary grades, most readers have enough of a task just to decode. Unless and until decoding is automatic, the reader cannot divert his or her brain to employing the strategies. The upper elementary grades are a good time to introduce the strategies and have students practice them to see how they work for *each student*. After that, we should suggest strategy use only if we find that they are needed for given readers on given texts. What we should be teaching students in middle school and beyond is this:

Comprehension is the result of active engagement in the text. There are three questions you need to keep in mind as you read:

1. Am I understanding what I'm reading?

2. How do I know? (And the answer to this is, *I can explain it in my own words, and I'm not afraid to answer questions about what it means.*)

3. What can I do when I don't understand what I'm reading?

This mindset is better than the insistence that students show proof in class that they have "used their strategies" when reading. It's similar to working through math problems. Students are encouraged to ask themselves if their answers to the problems make intuitive sense because we can get so lost inside the process that we take our eyes off the target: Does my answer even make sense?

Daniel Willingham gives us good advice about teaching with reading strategies (2006/2007, p. 7). His interpretation of the research and of the practices promoted by the National Reading Panel is that 1) reading strategies can only be applied when readers are decoding fluently, and 2) reading strategies, explicitly taught (named, modeled, practiced) in the upper elementary grades do offer a boost in comprehension, but 3) a limited number of sessions ("around six") does the trick. Therefore, extended sessions in explicitly teaching (naming, modeling, practicing) reading comprehension strategies year after year into middle and even high school is not productive, and detracts from fluency and concentration. Furthermore, Willingham asserts that the reason why comprehension does not improve with increased conscious practice of the strategies is that the strategies are in fact not skills (which would improve with practice year after year). Rather, says Willingham, "It [a reading comprehension strategy] may be more like a trick in that it's easy to learn and use, and the only difficulty is to consistently remember to apply it. An analogous process may be checking one's work in mathematics. There is not a lot to learn in checking your work: it's not a skill that requires practice. But you do have to remember to do it. Checking your work is analogous to reading strategies in another way. Checking your work will make it more likely that you get a problem right, but it doesn't tell you how to solve the problem. Similarly, reading comprehension strategies don't get reading comprehension done. They encourage the student to apply reading comprehension processes. If the comprehension processes can't do the job, reading strategies won't help much. For example, in order to 'summarize,' you need to comprehend enough to differentiate the main idea from subordinate ideas; for 'comprehension monitoring' to be useful, not only do you need to be able to recognize that you don't understand a passage, but also to be able to comprehend the material when you reread it" (p. 44)

So, yes, we should incorporate explicit instruction of known reading strategies such as those promoted by Zimmerman and Hutchens (2003), Beers (2003), Tovani (2004), and others. But explicit instruction alone will not create great readers. Readers become better readers through reading. Accessibility of interesting reading material and the opportunity to read it is our strongest game.

Bathwater: The Reading Standards are your One-Stop-Shop for college and career readiness.

Baby: The Common Core Reading Standards emphasize slow and recursive reading of serious, complex texts. But there is more to authentic reading than is dreamt of in its philosophy. The Reading Standards do not address other modes of functional reading. These are skimming (getting the gist of a text by flying over it, as you would if you were overviewing a textbook chapter), scanning (searching for specific information, as you might if you were looking for the answer to an end-of-chapter question), or sampling (reading a little of this and a little of that as we jump from one text to another, as we do so often when reading from the Internet). The closest we come to these other modes of reading is in Reading Standard 5, which is about text structures. Knowing how a text is organized helps us get to where we want to be quickly. Activities such as scavenger hunts in the library (or online), guided practice in reading a textbook chapter to review for a test, and timed quick reads to see what you remember are not included in the Reading Standards even though they strengthen skills that are needed in authentic reading situations.

Bathwater: The Common Core is directed at low-performing districts, mostly in "problem" districts. We don't have to worry about the Common Core in a "district like ours" where most of our graduates go to college.

Baby: While most districts do not have statistics about the number of their graduates who follow through on their college plans, all we need to do to see the need for the Common Core Standards, even in affluent districts, is to look at the results of the first Common Core English Language Arts (and Math) tests given for grades 3–8 in 2013. While the results in the major urban centers of New York State were even more dismal than expected, the results in the state's top-performing schools were significantly lower than expected. Any school district that remains complacent about the instructional implications of the Common Core (i.e., elevating the level, amount, and range of reading, writing, and academic vocabulary) will surely fall short of neighboring districts that do make the necessary changes.

We move next to how our assessment practices need to align to the instructional implications of the Reading Standards.

4 | Assessments for the Reading Standards

Are students growing as readers? How can we tell? How do the Common Core Reading Standards call for a change in our assessment models? We just heard about the instructional shift into giving students cold readings to assess their comprehension skills, as opposed to our traditional reliance on tests that are based entirely on information that the student is expected to have learned through explicit instruction.

An eighth grade teacher whom I'll call Claudia once remarked to me: "I teach *Of Mice and Men*, and then I give a test on it. They have my notes. They have my study guides. They participate in discussion groups. But all they're showing me on the test is that they can give back what I gave them in the first place. I don't know if they are becoming better readers or not." This teacher makes a really good point, so let's explore the kinds of assessments we do on assigned readings, what information we are deriving from our assessments, and how to achieve better alignment between our goals, our instruction, our assessment, and our response to assessment.

We're going to be talking about three kinds of assessment:

1. The "Reading Check" Quiz
2. The "Unit Test"
3. The "Cold Reading"

The first two kinds of assessment are traditional, familiar, and expected. It is that third kind, the "Cold Reading," that marks a real difference between what we've been doing and what we need to do now that the Common Core is in place.

The "Reading Check" Quiz: *Did You Read the Assigned Pages?*

The first and most basic kind of reading assessment is what I'm calling the "reading check" quiz. The purpose of the reading check quiz is to find out whether or not students have done the assigned reading. In a perfect world, this step would not be necessary, and maybe your students can be relied upon to do their assigned readings without your having to prod them by giving a reading check quiz. Although some of my students were independently conscience like that, most, even in advanced classes, did not have that level of discipline toward their academic studies. They needed to know that there was a good chance that they would be quizzed on their reading.

But that is not to say that they actually did the reading diligently. Many would do an end run around the text by reading the study guides, synopses, summaries, and even sample tests available online. As a teacher, it's tricky to thread the needle between giving a quiz whose questions don't require actual reading and giving a quiz whose questions are unreasonably detailed. Let's look at some possibilities, at two different levels of text complexity.

First, let's look at what a reading check quiz might look like for a small sample from Christopher Paul Curtis's *The Watsons Go to Birmingham—1963* (1995). This is the point in the story where the narrator wakes up on the Sunday morning, ready for church, and hears the shocking news that the church has just been bombed. He is hearing this news from his brother Byron, whom he calls By.

I ran to the door and into the house and By almost knocked me over running back toward the bedroom.

"What's wrong with Momma?" I asked.

I looked in the living room but Momma and Dad weren't there. I ran back to the bedroom, where Byron was trying to wrestle into a pair of pants.

"By! What happened?"

He got the pants up and said, "A guy just came by and said somebody dropped a bomb on Joey's church." And he was gone, exploring out of the front door trying to zip up his pants at the same time he ran off the porch. Some of the time I wondered if something really was wrong with me. Byron had just told me that someone had dropped a bomb on Joey's church, hadn't he? If that was true why did I just stand there looking stupid? If that was true why was I only thinking about how much trouble By was going to be in when they heard how loud he'd slammed the screen door, and asking myself why hadn't he put on his shoes? His socks wouldn't last two minutes on the Alabama mud.

I ran out onto the porch and into the street. It looked like someone had set off a people magnet, it seemed like everyone in Birmingham was running down the street, it looked like a river of scared brown bodies was being jerked in the same direction that By had gone, so I followed.

I guess my ears couldn't take it so they just stopped listening. I could see people everywhere making their mouths go like they were screaming and pointing and yelling but I didn't hear anything. I saw

Momma and Dad and Byron holding on to each other, all three of them looking like they were crazy and trying to keep each other away from the pile of rocks that used to be the front of the church.

Momma was so upset that she even forgot to cover the space in her front teeth. I couldn't hear her but I'd bet a million dollars she was shouting, "Why?" over and over like a real nut. It looked like Dad's mouth was yelling, "Joetta!" (pp. 183–4)

This is a key moment in the novel, so you can be sure students could easily find out about it by reading a synopsis. A question that asked *What happened at the church?* or *What kind of building was bombed?* would not reveal whether the student read the novel or just grabbed a synopsis. A question that asked students to recall whether Byron was struggling with his pants or a shirt or a shoelace or socks would be too detailed. However, it *is* significant that Byron was in such a panic over the bombing that he ran out of the house insufficiently dressed. The references to the pants, shoes, and socks are examples of the maxim *show, don't tell*, a maxim that is a hallmark of good storytelling: *use visuals to express what characters are feeling.* So the following would be a good and fair question to determine if a student had read this passage:

Which of the following visuals does the author use to express how Byron is feeling when he hears about the bombing of the church?

1. He runs out of the house still zipping his pants up, shoeless.
2. He says: "Oh, no! What a terrible disaster! The church has been bombed!"
3. He hides in the basement.
4. He exits the house cautiously and slowly, looking around for possible danger.

Two reasons might explain why a student would not select the first choice as the answer. The first reason is that the student did not read the text, and that fact would be revealed in wrong answers to similar questions. The second is that the student does not yet understand that authors provide visual details for good reason: to activate the "movie of the mind" in which the reader is expected to make inferences based on observable behavior, just as we do in real life. This is a question that addresses *Reading Standard 1: Read closely to determine what the text says explicitly and **to make logical inferences from it;** cite specific textual evidence when writing or speaking to support conclusions drawn from the text.*

Reading check quizzes should serve not only as a way of keeping students on the straight and narrow of doing their homework, but also as formative assessment: What do students' answers to direct comprehension questions tell us about the reading skills that need work? We can make such determinations by asking different kinds of questions that hit various Reading Standards.

Tip

Now is the time to refurbish the reading check quizzes that you've been giving to align them to the Reading Standards. Reading check quizzes should focus on Reading Standards 1, 2, and 3, with a dash of 5 and 6.

For example, Reading Standard 6 requires that students learn to "Assess how point of view or purpose shapes the content and style of a text." A not-so-good reading check question would ask students to identify that the passage above is told through the first person point of view of Daniel Watson. That fact alone is not specific to this passage. But the question that emanates from Reading Standard 6 cannot be, *How does point of view or purpose shape the content and style of this passage?* That is much too abstract. Students who know the answer won't understand the question. Try this:

> *In the moments that followed the bombing of the church, many disturbing details attracted Daniel's attention. Daniel is a child. If you were reading this passage and you didn't know that he was a child, what is* one *detail that he notices that might let you know that the description of the church bombing is being observed through a child's eyes, as opposed to the eyes of an adult?*

Daniel clearly does not absorb the gravity of the situation. In his child-like way, he follows his brother and the crowd, with no plan, just a child's trust, driving him. Several answers are possible, so the question is not unreasonably detailed. We want to see if 1) the students read the passage, and 2) they understand that the author is presenting a serious event through the eyes of a child.

Creating a reading check assessment that aligns to the Reading Standards is not easy, but the task is made easier if we focus on certain kinds of questions. Figure 4.1 offers some guidelines.

When composing reading check quiz questions, think about what active readers do: Readers visualize. Readers get to know characters, including what they say and how they say it. Readers know what the author emphasizes. Readers know details that cannot be found in a synopsis.

But it is not fair to expect readers to remember everything. In a reading check quiz, you might want to give some leeway, such as overlooking one wrong answer out of ten, so that an 80 becomes a 90 and so forth. No one remembers everything they read, and, after all, your purpose is to keep the students on track and doing their assigned reading with a reasonable amount of conscientiousness.

When students are reading books of choice from your list of recommendations, you can give generic reading check questions, such as the ones in Figure 4.2.

Guidelines for Creating Reading Check Assessments
Aligned to the Common Core

1. *Do not* ask questions that could be answered by reading a synopsis rather than the text.

2. *Do* ask questions that involve recall of a detail that is mentioned more than once, or that is described in vivid detail.

3. *Do not* ask questions that require recall of a single detail that was mentioned only once.

4. *Do* ask questions that involve dialogue and exact quotations by a character. Attentive readers can identify what characters said and did not say.

5. *Do* ask questions about what characters say about each other.

6. *Do* ask questions about physical things, especially hand-held items, that are referred to in the text.

Figure 4.1

Generic Reading Check Questions When Students
Are Not All Reading the Same Book

Literary Text:

1. Ask students to **name three hand-held items** that were mentioned in their books. Ask them to name the item, briefly describe it, name the character(s) who held the item, and briefly tell what was done with the item. The value of this question as a reading check assessment is that it reveals whether students paid attention to details, visualized, and understand how concrete items are used to advance the story. Often, students will find that these hand-held items have significance that transcends their practical use. In other words, they are symbols. For example, in the story *Julie of the Wolves* (Jean Craighead George), at one point the main character, Miyax, who is all alone, lost in the Arctic wilderness after having run away from home, uses many hand-held items that have significance beyond their obvious utility: Miyax sleeps with a chatty letter from a friend all about a dreamed-about trip to San Francisco. Miyax tucks this letter under her cheek as she falls asleep, a gesture that symbolizes her need to connect with her former life.

2. Ask students to draw, label, and explain in sentences any **geometric shape that represents a point in the story.** Remember that you are not asking them to draw a picture of something in the story. The purpose of the geometric representation is to show understanding of relationships within the story. Their representation can represent characters, settings, or both.

3. Ask students to compose six content-based questions that capture their reading assignment. These questions can be *Who? What? When? Where? Why? How?* They should answer their own questions, and their questions need to span the page range of the reading assignment.

Informational Text: Question types 2 and 3 above are applicable to informational text.

Figure 4.2

To assure that you are assessing for the targeted behavior (*Did you read the assigned pages?*), you should model these techniques in class before giving them as quiz items. You don't have to give all three. Any one of these will serve as a quick reading check assessment.

The Unit Test

Assessment based on instruction: Did you pay attention in my class?

Let's come back to Claudia's observation about her assessment for *Of Mice and Men*. Having done her job of "teaching *Of Mice and Men*," she now gives a unit test that gathers everything together: the plot, the themes, the characters, the vocabulary, the author background, the literary devices, the key quotations. Whew! It will be a full period test consisting of a matching column (matching characters to snippets of text that describe them—"We went over this."), multiple choice questions addressing events, literary devices ("We spent a lot of time on that."), causes and effects within the story, one or two questions about the kinds people and places that John Steinbeck is known for ("They had to read the bio that was in the book."), a vocabulary gap-fill using sentences extracted from the novel and a word bank in which the students do not have to change the forms of the words ("to make it easy, because they get all confused when you tell them they have to change the form to fit the words in"), and a one-paragraph essay asking whether George "had a choice" about killing his friend ("We held a debate on that.")

All in all, this is considered a "fair" test by the teacher, the students, the administration, and the parents. After all, it reflects everything this teacher taught over the three weeks in which *Of Mice and Men* was the centerpiece of her English class. If students read the book, took notes, paid attention to whole class instruction, participated in cooperative learning groups, answered their study guide questions, and reviewed everything the night before, they will ace Claudia's test, and their efforts, and hers, will be rewarded.

But something is missing, and Claudia knows it: What does a student's performance on a traditional literature test say about that student's growth as a reader? Not much. The paradigm that we're used to in English class is that we do whatever we can to reveal all we can about a particular work of literature. We teach *this* work of literature, *these* vocabulary words, *these* examples of figurative language, *these* universal themes, *these* turning points, conflicts, inferences, descriptions, and character webs. We show the movie, not because it improves reading comprehension, but because it will help students "get into the story," "visualize," and "enjoy it more." Maybe we assume that the ability to fare well on a test that asks for nothing more than recall of explicit instruction will transfer to better reading comprehension, but we have no empirical reason to think so, based on this model.

The *Did-you-pay-attention-in-my-class?* model has its value. After all, what you taught them, whether explicitly or through inductive reasoning and discussion, is important. *Of Mice and Men* is a must-read book, a part of the literary canon and American culture. But the traditional unit test does not tell you *whether students are becoming better readers.*

Yet, we cannot replace the traditional test-on-a-book with a test of comprehension of new text. Riots would break out: "Unfair! Unfair! You tested on something you never taught!" And if all of your efforts to illuminate themes, spotlight pivots in character development, make connections, and give notes were not going to show up later on a test, you might as well just post yourself on YouTube because your students are not going to be motivated by the sheer joy of literary wisdom that you dispense. There has to be a test on the book. You have to prepare them accordingly.

But where the Common Core Learning Standards come in is that next step, the one we usually don't take: *Are the students growing as readers? Are they developing their abilities so they can read increasingly complex text? How would they handle a new text, one that they have not seen before?* These questions lead us to the kind of assessment that creates the need for an instructional shift:

The "Cold Reading" Test

Are You Growing as a Reader?

To determine whether her students have become stronger readers as a result of her instruction, Claudia needs baseline information that comes from a pretest that uses a passage of comparable complexity to *Of Mice and Men.* The pretest asks Standards-based questions. Claudia will choose the following passage from *East of Eden* by John Steinbeck:

> Sometimes a kind of glory lights up the mind of a man. It happens to nearly everyone. You can feel it growing or preparing like a fuse burning toward dynamite. It is a feeling in the stomach, a delight in the nerve, of the forearms. The skin tastes the air, and every deep-drawn breath is sweet. Its beginning has the pleasure of a great stretching yawn; it flashes in the brain and the whole world glows outside your eyes. A man may have lived all his life in the gray, and the land and trees of him dark and somber. The events, even the important ones, may have trooped by faceless and pale. And then—the glory—so that a cricket

song sweetens the ears, the smell of the earth rises changing to his nose, and dappling light under a tree blesses his eyes. Then a man pours outward, a torrent of him, and yet he is not diminished.

Reading Standard 4 requires students to "Interpret words and phrases as they are used in a text, including determining technical, connotative, and figurative meanings, and analyze how specific word choices shape meaning or tone." This calls for a question about diction—word choice. It isn't so much a question about what an unfamiliar word might mean. If a student read the above passage having already known the meaning of the word *somber*, we cannot conclude anything about that student's ability to figure out a word through context. If your vocabulary question asks about the meaning of a word that a student already knows, you can't assess growth as a reader. You have no way of knowing if the student used context clues to figure out the meaning of a previously unknown word. Besides, most authors do not provide enough context clues to figure out a word the first time the reader encounters it. The author uses words assumed to be known by the reader. A good question on a reading check quiz for the above passage might reveal whether the student understands that the author has created a contrast between images of light and dark to represent life before and after the revelation that is the main idea of this passage.

Reading Standard 2 is about recognizing main ideas (aka central themes) and supporting details. Reading Standard 5 is about understanding the structure of a text. In this passage, the main idea is stated directly as the first sentence and restated, more dramatically, in the last sentence. A Standards-based question for Reading Standard 2 might ask the student to identify the sentence in the passage that states the main idea, as opposed to the details (*the skin, the taste, the forearms*). A question for Reading Standard 5 might reveal whether the student understands the "sandwich" structure of the passage—the main idea is stated as the first sentence, recapped in the last, and clarified by details in between.

Reading Standards-based questions align to Standards 1–6, although there is overlap. However, all the while, they are actually testing for Reading Standard 10, which is about reading *complex text independently*. (Reading Standards 7, 8, and 9 involve building knowledge or insight by integrating more than one text or medium.)

The only way to determine if students have become better readers is to measure their growth in comprehension on comparable text, not on the same text that has already been sliced and diced for them. This will be unsettling for students and parents who expect the content of tests to be available to students so they can memorize information. Under the Common Core philosophy, tests (not only on literary text, but also for history, social studies, science, and technical subjects) should include cold readings of passages on the grade level complexity bands to assess not only memorized information but also skill as a reader.

Tip

Assess comprehension, not strategies. Because direct instruction in reading strategies is considered important in many schools, some teachers have taken to assessing for the use of the strategies as ends in themselves. This is not a good idea. The only thing that counts in reading is comprehension. Strategies are a means to an end: In the fourth, fifth, and sixth grades, we can teach (i.e., name them, model them, practice them) a few strategies at each grade level. After that, we don't have to teach the strategies all over again. We certainly should not be assessing students on the use of them. Our time is better spent on analytical lessons that build the skills of reading complex text and building background knowledge, and responding to Standards-based questions (Willingham, 2006/2007).

A Close Look at Teaching Each of the Reading Standards

5 The Need for Phonics Instruction with Academic Reading

Before we get into each standard, I want to talk about the need for a phonics instruction—a certain kind of phonics instruction—at the upper elementary and secondary levels. What we have are long words and strange letter combinations, both of which can be very daunting to students in the secondary grades even though they are fluent readers of everyday language. Decoding (the mechanical process of mentally translating an arbitrary code of squiggles into meaningful sounds that we recognize as words) becomes increasingly demanding as we climb the grade levels and learning becomes more departmentalized. Students entering middle school and even high school still need instruction and practice to read technical language. That is because of a characteristic in the English language that I like to call the Scrabble™ or, if you prefer, Words With Friends™ Rule: The most common words in English tend to be made of, well, the most common letters, the ones with the fewest points in word games that reward the use of rare letters. Once you start making words with letters like X, Z, Q, K, J— you're getting higher points because the words *themselves* are rarer, that is to say, requiring more sophisticated word knowledge by the player. The most common words also tend to be short. When we start getting into the four-and-more syllable range, that's where the less familiar, more specific, and/or more abstract words are found. It isn't that such words are harder to learn, necessarily. *It is that inexperienced readers of academic text are not accustomed to seeing them and therefore don't know how to break them down.* That is where the "academic phonics" instruction comes in.

But there's good news: The longer the word, the more likely it is that we can break it down into known parts. Those components can help us figure out the meaning of other long words. That is because the longer the word, the more likely it is that it is derived from Latin and/or Greek (It's hard to tell the difference, as Greek bled into Latin, which bled into French, which bled into English. Many words, like people, have a family tree in which the roots and branches are entangled with those of other trees and clinging vines.)

There's a reason why technical words and words about language and thinking are derived from Greek. It goes back to the Renaissance. Long story short: The Latins cherry-picked fancy words from the Greeks to achieve sophistication, just as the Anglo Saxons adopted French borrowings to signify rising status. And, no, it's not that simple: The ideas blooming in the Renaissance required new words to name and shape them, and it just so happened that the Greek scholars in exile, after the fall of the Byzantine Empire, had both heady ideas and words to name them. ". . . the revival of Greek learning in Western Europe, which began to be felt in England soon after the commencement of the 16th century, opened a new source from which the English vocabulary could be enriched. Long before this time the language contained a certain number of Greek words, which had come in through the medium of Latin. And nearly all these Latinized Greek words had been adopted into all the languages of Europe and were extensively used in the language of science" (Papanis, n.d.). If you know that there's a reason and a pattern for the mystifying letter combinations that we find in the words of science and technology (but not often elsewhere in the language, hence their strangeness), then you feel more on solid ground with it, less at the mercy of some random chaotic force that created weird words just to make you feel helpless. Remember, humans have a strong need to make sense of things that appear disorderly. Our favorite way to make sense of things is to find reasons and patterns.

So what? Well, the preponderance of Greek-derived words in glossaries invites attention. Wouldn't the whole enterprise of teaching academic vocabulary be easier if students were less flummoxed by the tongue-twisting letter combinations that typify this level of language? And it's not just a matter of *bio-* means life; *-ology* means the study of (which, more accurately, means a *branch of knowledge*).

The instructional implication is simple:

1. Learn as many word components as you can. This means recognizing their forms and variations, knowing their meanings, and being able to generate as many examples as possible. The examples that you give to students should include familiar words as well as new words.

2. In your explanation of a new, long, or phonetically-challenging word, pronounce that word aloud repeatedly in your explanation.

3. In your explanation of a word, show its various forms: If it is a noun, or can be made into a noun, does it have a plural form? Can it be used as a verb, what are its forms? Is it an adjective, or can it be made into an adjective? Does it have an adverbial form?

4. Emphasize patterns and letter combinations: "This is one of those words where the *ch* is pronounced as k, as in *school*."

5. Show how the word divides into syllables, and how some of the syllables are morphemes (units of meaning: prefixes, roots, suffixes)

6. Make friends with your favorite unabridged dictionary and start excavating. Go beyond the definition, into the etymology at the end of each entry. There, you will find out how words are related and how to teach them through clusters and associations.

That's all there is to embedding phonics instruction into subject area teaching. It's really just a matter of including information about word structure and patterns in your explanation of a technical term.

Reading Standards 1–3

Key Ideas and Details

Standards 1–3 are about understanding the stated and implied meaning of the text and being able to sort out its central ideas from the supportive details. These are the skills of reading that most teachers already think of when they work toward comprehension. Although these Reading Standards are already in place, the difference in the Common Core lies in the increasing level of complexity in the text.

In this chapter:

Reading Standard 1: Close Reading

Reading Standard 1: Read closely to determine what the text says explicitly and to make logical inferences from it; cite specific textual evidence when writing or speaking to support conclusions drawn from the text. (www. corestandards.org/ELA-Literacy/CCRA/R/1)

> ## Tip
>
> Keep some perspective: Where have students been, prior to Grade 4?
>
> Grade 3: Literary and Informational: Ask and answer questions to demonstrate understanding of a text, referring explicitly to the text as the basis for the answers.
>
> Where are students expected to go, after Grade 8?
>
> Grades 9–10: Literary and Informational: Same as Grade 8.

Reading Standard 1 for Literary Text

For both literary and informational text, Reading Standard 1 requires that students be able to *prove their claims about the meaning of the text.* You can prove your claims about the meaning of the text without having to read closely if the text is simple for the reader. But making claims about meaning and proving them with textual evidence on simple text is not the point: The point is to untangle the meaning of text that is complex enough to require *close* reading, which entails building levels of understanding by rereading and really thinking about the explicit information and implications.

Your union representative is helping you figure out if you qualify for extended childcare leave, according to your contract. The relevant contractual clause states: "The superintendent must approve all written requests for paid or unpaid leave that are submitted thirty days or more prior to the first day of the requested leave." You ask your rep how the word must *is interpreted: Does that mean that the superintendent has to say yes to my leave as long as I request it thirty days ahead, or does it mean that the superintendent is the one who has to approve the leave, but they can say no? Does thirty days mean thirty school days? What if there's a snow day in there? Does that count? What if*

I submitted it exactly thirty days before I want my leave to start? This is a close read that depends upon the meaning of non-technical words (i.e., *must, days*). To find out, you rely on an expert in a labor contract, your union rep. If she has experience, her answer is credible based on precedents, or her training, or both.

An actor is working on his audition for the role of Macbeth. *He's deciding which words to emphasize within the rhythm of iambic pentameter; how long the pauses should be, considering the punctuation in the folio that the director has chosen. His acting coach is helping him decide on the vocal and physical qualities that will most accurately portray the feelings and intentions of the character as he speaks his words.* This is a close reading based on how to make words come alive via the human voice and body, taking every advantage of not only the words but also their sounds, rhythms, and groupings.

A student needs to translate a word problem into an algebraic equation. She needs to determine the role of each of several quantities, attending to only the relevant ones, converting each of the relevant quantities into a symbol, and then organize the symbols into a meaningful algebraic sentence before she can solve the problem. This is a close reading based on evaluating what is relevant, what is not, and what is the relationship between the relevant quantities. This close reading then makes the abstract representation of the text possible.

A hobbyist in clothing design and construction lays out her pattern directions next to the unfolded fabric on her large open dining room table, which doubles as a fabric-cutting surface. Before every single step in making a lined jacket, she consults the pattern directions because she's learned from experience that if the project is to turn out looking like it does on the cover of the pattern envelope, every step must be meticulously followed, just as written. This is a close reading of technical, process-based text. The reader has to go back and forth from the project to the text, comprehending just enough at a time to execute a finite task. In such situations, some readers prefer to first read the whole process, and then go back to read each step as it needs to be performed.

A seventh grade teacher is teaching the poem "A Dream Deferred" by Langston Hughes. First, she teaches the word deferred *by giving several contexts in which it is used, and asking the students to hypothesize about its meaning. The students then verify their theories by consulting a dictionary and writing the definition in their own words. The teacher then plays the famous reading of the poem by Ruby Dee, asking the students to close their eyes as they listen. She then asks them to write three interesting words from the poem, leaving plenty of space around each of the words on their papers. She asks the students to form pairs and help each other to answer three questions, using a note-taking writing style (abbreviations OK, complete sentences not required, informal language OK). The questions: 1) What does this word make you think about? 2) What other words have a similar meaning? and 3) Why do you think the poet Langston Hughes chose to use this particular word, rather than another word with a similar meaning? She then convenes the class and asks students to speak out on their findings.*

She does this for five different words in the poem. She writes the five words on the board. Because the poem is built with metaphors, she writes the corresponding phrases ("raisin in the sun"; "fester like a sore"; "crust and sugar over like a syrupy sweet"; "sags like a heavy load"). She asks the class whether they think these metaphors are supposed to be positive or negative? She calls their attention to the image of a "syrupy sweet" getting them to see that, although this image, by itself, may evoke a positive reaction, in the context of the other negative images, including the verb "crust," it definitely is meant negatively, else it would not fit in with the other negative images, all leading up to the rage expressed in the final word "explode." She then has the students, in pairs, write an analysis of the poem in which they make a claim about the meaning of the poem and support their claim with evidence. This is a close reading of this short and unforgettable poem. Much more teaching can follow, including historical background (point of view), allusion (Lorraine Hansberry's *A Raisin in the Sun*), and how the ideas in the poem can be translated into another genre, such as a rap. But this close reading is accomplished through the exploration of the connotation of its metaphors.

In these examples, readers go over the text meticulously because they need to solve a problem: interpreting a contract, breathing life into a fictional character, using algebra, following technical directions to create something, accessing the author's intent. We can model strategies and follow protocols for close reading forever, but students will read analytically when they need the text to solve a problem. It's up to us, then, to devise problems that entail careful reading, i.e., dipping back into a text, puzzling through its problematical words, internal references, abstractions, assertions, and implications.

Do not confuse close reading with word-by-word reading. Proficient readers read by chunking related words, processing them as units of meaning. Language is understood through the relationships of words to each other and to the main idea, not through the meanings of individual words in isolation. Context delivers meaning. By that, I mean that context cuts down on the possibilities of meaning for any given word. In the sentence that you are reading now, you are not understanding the word *sentence* to mean a term of imprisonment because doing so would make no sense in this context. In this paragraph, when you encounter the word *mean*, you understand it in its intended context, not in a mathematical context or as a synonym for *cruel*. The theory of whole language is that meaning is derived more through context (hence, the primacy of background knowledge) than through the meaning of, or even the decoding of, individual words that the reader does not know. If it were necessary to know every word in a text *before* understanding it, no one would ever have been able to understand authentic language, language that introduces new words in context. In fact, being able to comprehend language despite its having unfamiliar words is the very way in which language grows. Stephen Krashen (1984) calls it the "input hypothesis," which means that humans grow their language knowledge because of (not in spite of) hearing new language that is nestled within comprehensible input: In understanding a compelling message, we pick up some of the new words that were used to deliver the message. Do that enough times, and we acquire more and more language. Given the opportunity to use new language in a non-threatening way, we promote words from the receptive (listening, reading) to the productive (speaking, writing) modes in our language storehouse.

The relevance of whole language theory to close reading of complex text is that we do not have to be taught every single word before we encounter it, nor do we have to stop-and-look-up unknown words the first time through. In 1983, Frank Smith wrote *Twelve Easy Ways to Make Learning to Read Hard and 1 Difficult Way to Make It Easy* in which he explains how knowing context helps readers unconsciously anticipate what words are likely to flow into the text, and what the author probably intends them to mean. "Fluent readers do not read words, they read meanings. Reading for meaning is far easier than reading words . . . We all know that when reading an unfamiliar or difficult text, whether a complex novel, a technical article, or something in a fairly unfamiliar foreign language, it is impossible to read and simultaneously refer to a dictionary, or to slog through the text a sentence at a time. We may be tempted to slow down, but the only efficient strategy is, in fact, to speed up, to read on. When it is necessary to 'read carefully' for one reason or another we do not try to do it cold. Instead we take a quick scan through the material 'to see what it is about'—which means to get the essence of the meaning—and then read through a second time, still relatively fast, to get the details." **"Slow reading" does not mean that we spend a long time going from one single word or sentence to the next. If we did that, we would never get the gist. If we don't get the gist, the details are meaningless. Slow reading means that we get the gist and then go back, either to clarify, or to build on our initial understanding, or both. Similarly, careful reading is not the same as cautious, or timid reading, which would be reading with the pervasive fear of making some kind of mistake. When it comes to close reading, the key is to reread, armed with awareness of the author's overall meaning.** According to Smith, "The best way to discover the meaning of a difficult passage is to read more of the passage. The best way to identify an unfamiliar word in the text is to draw inferences from the rest of the text. The best way to learn the strategies and models for identifying new words . . . is to read."

The brain wants to be efficient in receiving messages through language. To the brain, making sense of text is more important than finding errors. In fact, the brain is "annoyed" by errors in text that impede comprehension. To avoid such annoyances, the brain has a way of overriding mistakes (or even words that it does not comprehend) so that meaning can get through. To test that theory of how the brain functions, think about a time when you tried to proofread something that you wrote and didn't notice typos. You didn't notice them, not because you didn't know they were typos, but because your brain, in knowing what you meant, "auto-corrected" the obviously wrong spelling. In a kind of optical illusion, you "read" what you knew you meant. (That is why one technique of proofreading is to read the text from the bottom of the page up to the top. When you do that, you are less likely to anticipate what word comes next, more likely to read word by word: You won't comprehend very well, but you will notice errors.) By the way, the same phenomenon of "mental auto-correction" comes into play when we read our students' writing: Concentration on meaning detracts from finding mistakes that do not impede meaning. (In my early years of teaching, I was taken to task by a supervisor for failing to mark every error on student papers, when a set of graded papers was suddenly intercepted for the purpose of evaluating me as a writing teacher. I was "more careful" thereafter, until I developed the confidence and understanding that students do not benefit from having every single one of their errors pointed out anyway. We should respond to student writing in a way that will actually help them improve incrementally.)

Note

A reader's understanding of a bit of language in the text is informed by the whole, not so much the other way around. This argues for the process of reading quickly for the gist, and then rereading as many times as necessary, each time more slowly, to solve a given problem answerable by a deep understanding of the text.

And just why does purposeful rereading improve comprehension? Why can't we understand complex text fully if we concentrate hard enough on the first reading? The reason has to do with how the brain processes new information. Working memory is the "place" where moment-by-moment information is processed. But the brain can only store five to seven unrelated bits of information at a time in working memory. When you read seven contiguous words, you don't process them word by word. Rather, your brain unifies (chunks) phrases as single units of meaning. But your brain won't do that unless the phrases are familiar. Rereading creates familiarity, and thus improves the brain's ability to process multiple words (phrases and clauses) as single units, units that can grow larger with each reading. After several readings, the word groupings that your brain can process as single units grow larger, so that your brain can actually process more information as one related concept that, in turn, hooks onto other related concepts, each of which consist of multiple words. Think of this like quilting: Small squares get sewn together to form larger squares, which are then less tedious to put together to create the whole quilt.

The Best Scaffolding Is Background Knowledge

A reader's ability to comprehend text improves with the reader's familiarity with its content, style, and form. That is why an architect can read a blueprint much faster and better than I can: Where I'm trying to make sense of lines of different thicknesses, she's already seeing whole rooms at a glance. Given two texts of equal complexity, one on a subject familiar to the reader and the other on an unfamiliar subject, any reader will show better comprehension on the familiar subject. This is obvious, but I mention it to reinforce the axiom that background knowledge is the most important determiner of comprehension on a given text. The instructional implication is that giving students background knowledge accomplishes more than any graphic organizer, reading strategy (other than rereading), set of questions, or highlighter. However, let's not confuse background knowledge with an explanation of the actual text that obviates the need to read it. Although we want students to, in the words of the Common Core, "grapple with" complex text, we can give them easier reading material and pictures that build the background knowledge they will need to read a particular piece.

The need for background knowledge (both in vocabulary and information) argues strongly for having students read their books of choice as part of their school experience. Trying to get students to do close reading of challenging text without their building up their reading muscles on their own by pursuing their own interests will simply not work. Lucy Calkins (Calkins, Ehrenworth, and Lehman, 2012, p. 45) stresses the importance of formative assessment. She strongly advocates that teachers keep running records of the books and articles that students are choosing for independent reading. "All too frequently, we have seen teachers conducting running records or other assessments just at one or two points during the school year, and not dreaming of accelerating progress save at those intervals. If readers are advancing on course, they are probably moving up three text levels a year during many years, and readers who enter the school year well below level might progress as many as five or six levels in a single year." Stephen Krashen (n.d.) makes the case for what he calls "narrow reading," lots of reading about a favorite topic, as opposed to reading a variety of not-so-favorite topics: "The case for narrow reading is based on the idea that acquisition of both structure and vocabulary comes from many exposures in a comprehensible text, that is, we acquire new structures and words when we understand messages, many messages, that they encode." Narrow reading, according to Krashen, provides built-in review of the language of the topic. And we need not worry that habitual reading about a single subject will provide non-transferable knowledge: "Deep reading in any topic will provide exposure to a tremendous amount of syntax and vocabulary that is used in other topics." If middle and high school teachers make the time for students to read books and articles of choice, the reward will be that many students will be motivated to read more, and to read more complex text on their own. If that were to happen, our troubles would be over.

OK, Let's Try This Highlighter Thing Again

Literacy expert Tim Shanahan advocates an analytical approach to complex text that brings text at the frustration level into the student's instructional level. Up to this point, I've been making the case for rereading as the main strategy in close reading. But I realize that sometimes readers need to dig into individual sentences with mental pick-axes, sifters, and earth-movers to separate the dross from the gold and see what's what. Enter the much-abused highlighter.

Most students end up highlighting way too much of the text. Not helpful. What Shanahan suggests is that we teach students to unpack meaning in text by seeing how the parts connect. Nouns, verbs, adjectives, and adverbs are the "bricks" of language: these kinds of words deliver meaning. Conjunctions, pronouns, conjunctive adverbs (*however, moreover, therefore,* etc.) and, to a lesser extent, prepositions, are the "mortar," the words that connect, represent, and contextualize the content-bearing words, creating a cohesive structure. Hence, these parts of speech are called *structure class words.* Picture a school dance in the 1950s. The potential dancers are not dancing yet. They are lined up against the wall, boys on one side, girls on the other. That is what the nouns, verbs, adjectives, and adverbs look like before the structure class words get everybody up and dancing. The structure class words are like the music and the dance itself. To use another metaphor, the structure class words are the backstage crew. They don't get to take a bow, but without them, the actors would wander aimlessly in the dark.

Complex text is often highly self-referential. By that, I mean that the text contains many words that refer to or represent other words and concepts within the text, sometimes nearby, sometimes several words or even several sentences removed. Let's refer to these words as connectives, and let's include punctuation as a connective as well.

Enter the highlighter. But this time, the highlighter's job is more specific than just "highlight the important points" and less abstract than "highlight the key words." What we're going to do is to highlight some of the structure words so we can see what they refer to, what they connect, what they represent. Let's see how such highlighting might look if applied to a passage in *The Adventures of Tom Sawyer* (Twain, 1998, p. 137):

At last the sleepy atmosphere was stirred, and vigorously. The murder trial came on in the court. It became the absorbing topic of village talk immediately. Tom could not get away from it. Every reference to the murder sent a shudder to his heart, for his troubled conscience and fears almost persuaded him that these remarks were put forth in his hearing as "feelers"; he did not see how he could be suspected of knowing anything about the murder, but still he could not be comfortable in the midst of this gossip. It kept him in a cold shiver all the time. He took Huck to a lonely place to have a talk with him. It would be some relief to unseal his tongue for a little while, to divide his burden of distress with another sufferer. Moreover, he wanted to assure himself that Huck had remained discreet.

Now let's highlight some connectives:

At last the sleepy atmosphere was stirred, and vigorously. The murder trial came on in the court. **It** *became the absorbing topic of village talk immediately. Tom could not get away from* **it.** *Every reference to the murder sent a shudder to his heart, for his troubled conscience and fears almost persuaded him that these remarks were put forth in his hearing as "feelers"; he did not see how he could be suspected of knowing anything about the murder, but still he could not be comfortable in the midst of* **this** *gossip.* **It** *kept him in a cold shiver all the time. He took Huck to a lonely place to have a talk with him. It would be some relief to unseal* **his** *tongue for a little while, to divide* **his** *burden of distress with another sufferer.* **Moreover,** *he wanted to assure himself that Huck had remained discreet.*

We want students to understand that the pronouns *it* and **this** as highlighted above, refers to the gossip about the murder, and that the two highlighted pronouns **his** refer to Tom, as opposed to Huck. (Whenever two people of the same gender are referred to by the same pronoun, it is possible to confuse one for the other.) The word **moreover,** a conjunctive adverb, creates the relationship between Tom's main reason for meeting with Huck and the secondary reasons that were just mentioned.

Let's try another. This is a passage from *The Scarlet Letter* (Hawthorne, 2002). This time, we'll use a question-and-answer format to focus attention on the words that represent other words in the text:

(1) "On the wall hung a row of portraits, representing the forefathers of the Bellingham

(2) lineage, some with armour on their breasts, and others with stately ruffs and robes of

(3) peace. All were characterized by the sternness and severity which old portraits so

(4) invariably put on, as if they were the ghosts, rather than the pictures, of
departed

(5) worthies, and were gazing with harsh and intolerant criticism at the pur-
suits and

(6) enjoyments of living men."

> Line 2: To what do the words *some* and *others* refer?
>
> Line 3: If there were a word or phrase following the word *all*, what might
> that be?
>
> Line 4: To what does the word *they* refer?

One more, and this time we're going to connect the subject to the verb to make
meaning from a sentence that takes some side trips away from that essential
relationship. You may recognize this sentence:

"When in the course of human events it becomes necessary for one people
to dissolve the political bands which have connected them with another and to
assume among the powers of the earth, the separate and equal station to which
the Laws of Nature and Nature's God entitle them, a decent respect to the
opinions of mankind requires that they should declare the causes that compel
them to the separation."—The Declaration of Independence, Thomas Jefferson

There are lots of thickets and brambles in this great sentence in which
unwary readers can entangle themselves, but let's look at it when the subject-
verb of the main clause is highlighted:

"When in the course of human events it becomes necessary for one people
to dissolve the political bands which have connected them with another and to
assume among the powers of the earth, the separate and equal station to which
the Laws of Nature and Nature's God entitle them, **a decent respect** to the opinions of mankind **requires** that they should declare the causes that compel them
to the separation.

Now we can ask: *A decent respect for what?* and *What does the decent respect require
us to do?*

The point is that there are two often overlooked tools that help us access
meaning in long, meandering sentences. The first is highlighting connective
words and asking ourselves what these words connect or represent. The second is stripping the sentence down to the subject-verb of the main clause. (The
subordinate—aka dependent—clause, if present, is signaled by a relative pronoun or subordinating conjunction, the most common of which are *as, after,
although, while, when, before, because, until, unless, since*.)

Standard 1 Summary

The term *close reading* refers to the process of acquiring subtle information about complex text. Readers should rely primarily on equipping themselves with relevant background knowledge and the patience to reread, each time with a more specific purpose. Sometimes, it may be necessary to activate the strategy of locating connective words (pronouns, conjunctions, conjunctive adverbs) and consciously matching them to their referents or noting exactly what elements they connect.

Guiding Questions for Readers: Standard 1

1. What does the text mean? How do I know?

2. What background knowledge do I need to understand what I'm reading? How can I obtain it at my level of understanding?

3. Am I having any problems understanding what the connective words refer to?

Reading Standard 2: Central Idea

Reading Standard 2: Determine central ideas or themes of a text and analyze their development; summarize the key supporting details and ideas. (www.corestandards.org/ELA-Literacy/CCRA/R/2)

Tip

Keep some perspective: Where have students been, prior to Grade 4?

Grade 3: Literary: Recount stories, including fables, folk tales, and myths from diverse cultures; determine the central message, lesson or moral and explain how it is conveyed through key details in the text.

Informational: Determine the main idea of a text; recount the key details and explain how they support the main idea.

Where are students expected to go, after Grade 8?

Grades 9–10: Literary: Determine the theme or main idea of a text and analyze in detail its development over the course of the text, including how it emerges and is shaped by the specific details; provide an objective summary of the text.

Informational: Determine the central idea of a text and analyze its development over the course of the text including how it emerges and how it is shaped and refined by specific details; provide an objective summary of the text.

Reading Standard 2 is essentially the same throughout the grade levels and for both literary and informational text. Text complexity is the variable going from one grade to the next. Every year, we are expected to work on the skill of finding the central idea and being able to summarize it, orally (Speaking and Listening Standard 2) and in writing (Writing Standard 2).

Reading Standard 2 breaks into three parts:

1. Determine the central ideas or themes of a text
2. Analyze the development of the central ideas or themes
3. Summarize the key supporting details and ideas

Reading Standard 2 differs significantly whether the text is literary or informational. Central ideas in informational text are usually stated directly and placed in predictable locations within the text. Themes in literary text may or may not be stated directly. When thematic statements are directly stated, whether through the mouths of characters or via the author (third person objective narrator), such statements may be placed anywhere in the text.

Reading Standard 2 for Literary Text

About Themes

The central idea in a novel, story, drama, or poem is often called the theme. The more complex a literary work is, the greater the number of themes that run through it. In fact, when we say that a work of literature is rich or layered, what we mean is that it expresses multiple themes.

A common inaccuracy regarding themes is that the theme of a literary work is some kind of single *lesson*—the "moral of the story," a "life lesson." Although fables, parables, and some simple stories do carry a clearly-defined moral lesson, more sophisticated literature is *not* so explicit, didactic, or limited. Rather, one of the great appeals of literature is that, like real life, characters, their decisions, and the results of these decisions are laced with ambiguity: the most interesting and complex characters and stories make us think and re-think. The meaning of a rich story grows in our eyes as our own life experiences change how we interpret characters and events. Literature generates discussion, speculation, disagreement, and even discomfort.

Your students have probably been taught that "theme" means "moral of the story." They need to learn that 1) not all stories come with a moral lesson, 2) the richer the story, the more themes it portrays, and 3) all pieces of the story, drama, or poem are relevant and connected to at least one of its themes.

A theme can be an observation about life, an observation that the author feels strongly about and wants you, as the reader, to think about also. Themes are pervasive, like a threads weaving through a work of literature. Because themes are abstractions, the ability to identify themes requires higher order thinking skills. Why don't authors just "come right out and tell you the theme?" Why do they make you work for it? The answer to this often-asked question is that, first of all, authors often do come right out and tell you the theme. They are likely to do so several times, to make sure that you get it.

In Harper Lee's *To Kill a Mockingbird* (1960), Atticus declares one of the key themes of the novel when he tells his children, "You never understand a person until you consider things from his point of view—until you climb into his skin and walk around in it" (Chapter 9). Later in that thematic chapter, Atticus, referring to the upcoming trial, which he knows to be a lost cause, tells the children: "Simply because we were licked a hundred years before we started is no reason for us not to try to win." And, in Chapter 10, upon granting his son his first rifle, a symbol of manhood in their culture, he advises solemnly: "Shoot all the bluejays you want, if you can hit 'em, but remember it's a sin to kill a mockingbird." Obviously, when a character or narrator speaks the title in context, it's a five-alarm Theme Alert.

In F. Scott Fitzgerald's *The Great Gatsby* (1925), first person narrator and sideline observer of the action in the story, Nick Carraway, shares with the reader a bit of his father's wisdom: "Whenever you feel like criticizing anyone," he told me, "just remember that not everyone has had the advantages that you've had" (Chapter 1). Nick's closing words to the reader capture the theme of trying in vain to re-create the past: "So we beat on, boats against the current, borne ceaselessly into the past."

And, in *Horton Hatches the Egg*, Dr. Seuss (Geiss, 1940), as the narrator, states the theme pretty explicitly with this emphatic statement of approval for rejecting the maternal rights of the runaway mother, the despicable bird Mayzie: "And it should be, it should be, it should be like that. Because Horton was faithful. He sat and he sat."

About Perceiving Themes

Identifying themes in literary text is a higher order thinking skill, calling for the ability to make inferences and to find commonalities in the details that the author chose to include. This skill calls for teasing out the difference between plot—the sequence of events themselves—and the ideas about life and human nature behind the plot.

Do all works of literature even have a theme? The answer would depend on how broadly we choose to define "theme," but all works of literature, however silly or shallow, are unified, if by nothing other than the series of mistakes in judgment made by the main character to drive the plot.

In literature, themes are hiding in plain sight: Authors tend to express their themes metaphorically, not to make them more difficult to perceive, but to make them more interesting, more powerful, more meaningful. Metaphors are memorable and strike us as true, even more than direct statements usually do. Aristotle attributed metaphor as a sign of true genius, positing that metaphors require an "eye for resemblance." It is this eye for resemblance that allows us to perceive themes: Readers (or viewers) have to be able to think comparatively to connect motifs (repeated images or references). Motifs always reveal theme.

When events or minor characters seem tangential, they often have thematic significance. That is why readers need to question why seemingly minor characters and events are included. If we accept that well-constructed literature does not fiddle around with unnecessary details, we can enrich our understandings by examining those little diversions that seem to wander from the main story.

Themes can be expressed by a single word. Abstract nouns are best. Because your students will probably look at you blankly if you ask them to capture the themes as abstract nouns, here is a list of noun endings that create abstract nouns, along with common literary themes that have these endings:

Abstract noun-making endings:

-ance	*-hood*	*-al*
-ence	*-ness*	*-ism*
-ity	*-ment*	*-tude*
-ty	*-tion*	
-ship	*-sion*	

These endings form an endless list of words that can express the meaningful experiences and observations that authors portray.

We may identify themes in simpler words that express abstract concepts as well: *love, hate, revenge, jealousy, adventure, honor, power, fear, death, loss,* etc. Themes may also be identified in terms of binary conflicts: *good vs. evil, survival vs. death, love vs. hate, nobility vs. corruption, power vs. weakness,* etc. And many teachers still rely on the three broad conflicts: *Human against human; human against nature; human against self.*

Themes may be expressed by a question: *What if . . . ? Why does . . . ? What is_____ like?* (See Figure 6.1.)

The important thing is that themes do not hide. We recognize themes in literature by their reappearance throughout the piece and by the amount of focus that the author places on certain details.

Questions to Help Identify Themes

1. What observations about life does the author seem to think are important?

2. What is the author trying to get us to notice and think about? If this piece of literature were a movie, what close-ups would we see? How do these close-ups connect to the abstract nouns or other nouns on our list?

3. What is the author repeating? Do events share anything in common?

4. What does the title mean? Is the title referred to explicitly in the text? If so, in what context? If not, why do you think the author chose this title?

Figure 6.1

Analyzing the Development of Themes

Reading Standard 2 requires that students go further than simply identifying themes: students need to track the development of those themes. This amounts to finding evidence that justifies our claims about themes. Such evidence can be found in literary elements, particularly characters, events (plot) and setting.

Themes and characters: What are the values of the main character? (What does the main character think is important? What does the main character feel strongly about and work to achieve? Why?) Consider the minor characters, who often serve a thematic purpose: How do the minor characters express the observations that the author is making about life and human nature?

Themes and events: How do the main characters respond to the events? What events in the story are planned and controllable, as opposed to those that are out of the control of the main characters? This is an important question because a common theme in literature is that our everyday lives get blown off-course by unpredictable events.

Themes and setting: Setting (time and place) can be geographical (a specific place on the map) or situational (high school, for example). In a novel such as Edith Wharton's *Ethan Frome* the setting (the barren, claustrophobic, hard-scrabble town of Starkfield, Massachusetts) embodies the themes of harshness and lovelessness. The setting can mirror the inner life of the main character; or, as with Thornton Wilder's *Our Town*, the setting can actually be a key theme.

Perceiving central ideas (themes) in literary text is the result of experience, awareness of what the author wants us to pay attention to, and, most of all, a search for clarity about how all of the pieces fit together, why all the pieces have been included.

> About Lyric Poetry: Poetry falls into two categories: narrative and lyric. Narrative poetry tells a story; lyric poetry expresses an idea or feeling. We find the themes in narrative poetry in the same way we find the themes in other stories. We find the themes in lyric poetry in a manner that is similar to how we find themes in informational text, i.e., by looking for repetition of words, phrases, and images.

Central Ideas in Informational Text

The central ideas in informational text are much easier to identify than themes in literary text. For one thing, informational text can be expected to develop a *single* idea. In a paragraph, that idea is likely to be explicitly stated in the form of a topic sentence. In a multi-paragraph passage, the central idea is the single idea that appears in every paragraph and in the majority of all of the sentences. In a book, the central idea will be laid out explicitly in the first chapter.

Visual metaphors (graphic organizers) can help students find central ideas: the umbrella, the tree, the tabletop supported by its legs.

Analyzing the Development of Central Ideas

It is important that students understand the difference between central ideas and supportive details. The following are types of supportive details, not main ideas:

- examples
- statistics
- anecdotes
- reasons
- cause and effect statements

When students can identify these supportive details, and color-coding them is a good way to do that, they can eliminate them as main ideas. In multiple choice questions, supportive details are always given as wrong answers, so it would be very helpful if students could respond to the choices by saying, "No, this one is an example, not a main idea; no, this one is a reason, not a main idea."

Descriptions, when they permeate the text, can be main ideas. So can extended definitions. The author's opinion can be a main idea. When it is, as in an editorial, expect the opinion to be stated in key places and repeated in different words throughout the editorial. Editorialists almost always end their pieces with main idea statements of opinion, leaving the reader with a powerful impression.

Tip

A classroom practice for finding central ideas in newspaper editorials: Students should read editorials. Reading editorials is important for analytical thinking, learning to construct a written argument (Writing Standard 1), and building awareness of local, national, and world events. Editorials are tailor-made for addressing Reading Standard 2 because of their predictable structure and repetition of the central idea, which may also be called a thesis statement. Most editorialists take no chances in having the reader miss the main point, so they restate it at least twice. The thesis of an editorial may appear in the opening paragraph. If it doesn't, that is probably because the editorialist is setting up the reader with either a scenario designed to evoke a strong reaction, or with background information. The thesis statement is usually stated explicitly at the end, and at various other points throughout the editorial. Give students an editorial and ask them to highlight *a* sentence (one of many—not *the* sentence) that expresses the main idea. Then, have them hold up their editorial, look around the room, and notice that other readers settled upon different statements as the main idea. By doing this, they will learn not only the main idea of that particular editorial, but also the reading comprehension skill of recognizing the reiteration of central idea in persuasive text.

Composing a Summary of Themes and Central Ideas

Writing a summary is a higher order thinking skill because it requires analysis and evaluation. Evaluation is required to select only the most important information for the summary. When students write a summary, they are addressing Writing Standard 2 ("Write informative/explanatory texts to examine and convey complex ideas and information clearly and accurately through the effective selection, organization, and analysis of content"; www.corestandards.org). When students verbalize a summary, they are addressing Speaking and Listening Standard 2 ("Integrate and evaluate information presented in diverse media and formats, including visually, quantitatively, and orally" (www.corestandards.org).

In summarizing literary text, most people will recount the main plot events in chronological order, or in the order in which the events unfolded in the story. That is fine if we want to stick to the level of the plot. If we were to summarize *The Watsons Go to Birmingham—1963* (Curtis, 1995), on the basis of plot only, we might say this: "*The Watsons Go to Birmingham—1963* is about an African American family that decides to go on a road trip from their home in Flint, Michigan, to visit relatives in Birmingham, Alabama. The real reason they are visiting the relatives is because Byron has been behaving badly and getting into trouble with bad friends. The parents think that if Byron lived with his grandmother, he would get away from the bad influences that are getting him into trouble. But in Birmingham there is a bombing of his grandmother's church because of racism. This was a real tragedy that happened in 1963. Four little girls died in the tragedy and two other girls were terribly injured. Byron's parents do not know how to explain the tragedy. Byron's younger brother Kenny explains it because he had run into the church to save his little sister. This book is about racism."

This summary certainly hits upon the theme of racism, but here is how the summary might sound if we dug more into the themes; we might focus on the settings (Flint, Michigan and Birmingham, Alabama) and the main characters. We might consider sentence frames that focus us on these elements:

In *The Watsons Go to Birmingham—1963*, Flint, Michigan, is a place where:

... a young teenager can start to take the wrong path and get into serious trouble.

... parents might decide to move their son to a completely different environment in the hope that he will not be exposed to bad influences.

... family members have to huddle close to each other in the winter because of the cold inside their apartments.

In *The Watsons Go to Birmingham—1963*, Birmingham, Alabama, is a place where:

... a church where African Americans worship can be bombed by racists who oppose civil rights.

... you might find out that violence can happen in the very place where you went to seek safety.

... parents can be at a loss to explain the violence of the world to their children.

Now, let's try it by focusing on a main character:

In *The Watsons Go to Birmingham—1963*, Kenny is bullied by his older brother Byron.

In *The Watsons Go to Birmingham—1963*, Byron is a worry to his parents, and for good reason.

In *The Watsons Go to Birmingham—1963*, Wilona (Momma) thinks that her own mother's ways with children will straighten Byron out.

The sentence frame that focuses on a literary element such as setting or character can bring us to the themes more than a recounting of the events can do. When we ask students to compose summaries of stories, which we should, we should provide instruction for including thematic statements emanating from characters and setting as well as recountings of plot events.

An effective technique for teaching summarizing informational text is to teach students to select from a short list of verbs and sentence frames: *The author explains . . . : The author describes . . . " The author defines . . .; The author compares . . . to . . . ;* These sentence frames focus the student on the author's purpose.

63

Tip

Students can address author's purpose by thinking like the author. Ask students to put themselves into the author's head before he or she decided to write whatever it is that you are reading. Get inside the author's thoughts by completing this frame: "I think I'll write a (fill in genre) about (word or phrase about the content). I want people to understand (here's your central idea or theme)."

Standard 2 Summary

Reading Standard 2, consistent throughout the grade levels, addresses the need for students to perceive main ideas and themes in literary and informational text, to be able to explain how the main ideas and themes are developed, and to summarize what they've read. To teach students to do this with increasingly complex text, you need to focus students on literary elements, repetition (restatement, reiteration), placement of main ideas in various genres, and the major patterns through which authors organize details in the service of their main ideas.

Guiding Questions for Readers: Standard 2

1. What might be a good title and sub-title for this text?

2. Usually, in informational text, the author expresses the main idea in one sentence; often the main idea is repeated in one or more other sentences in the text. Can you find one (or more) sentences that capture the main idea?

3. Pyramid: What do you think is the single most important word in this text? Write that word in the middle of the top of a piece of paper. Then, under that word, write three other important words from (different parts of) the text, across the page. Then, under those three words, write five other important words. You should now have a pyramid that takes up about two-thirds of the page. On the bottom of the page, write a sentence that expresses the main idea of the text. Use your main word and several of the other words in your sentence.

Reading Standard 3: Understand and Follow Progressions

Reading Standard 3: Analyze how and why individuals, events, and ideas develop and interact over the course of a text. (www.corestandards.org/ELA-Literacy/CCRA/R3)

Tip

Keep some perspective: Where have students been, prior to Grade 4?

Grade 3: Literary: Describe characters in a story (e.g., their traits, motivations, or feelings) and explain how their actions contribute to a sequence of events.

Where are students expected to go, after Grade 8?

Grades 9–10: Literary: Analyze how complex characters (e.g., those with multiple or conflicting motivations) develop over the course of a text, interact with other characters, and advance the plot or develop the theme.

Reading Standard 3 for literary text asks students to focus on the physical (as opposed to thematic) elements of a story, i.e., characters, setting, and events. As students move up through the grades, Reading Standard 3 requires that they not only describe characters, settings, and events, but also that they understand and explain how these three literary elements interact with each other to advance the story.

Reading Standard 3 for Literary Text

English teachers often use the terms *static characters* (those who remain the same throughout the story) and *dynamic characters* (those who change as a result of the events in the story). These are useful terms for Reading Standard 3. Since this Reading Standard focuses on progressive changes in a story, particularly in characterization, readers need to read with awareness of the relationship between events and characters: Which characters change after events? Why? How? How do we know?

To engage Reading Standard 3 in Grade 4, we need to focus students on finding evidence in the text that shows changes in a character: *Does a character change his or her mind? When? Why? How do we know? How does a character feel about a particular event in the story? How do we know?*

For Reading Standard 3, we're trying to help students recognize pivotal moments, those moments in the story when characters change internally as a result of how their situations change externally. Anyone can see, for example, that Huck Finn's daily life changes once he flees from danger on land and joins up with Jim on the river: He no longer lives in Miss Watson's house, no longer goes to school, no longer hangs out with Tom and the boys, and, of course, no longer is imprisoned by his abusive father. Those are all external changes. But Huck's gradual internal change—revealed incrementally in his own words— has to do with his slow and unsteady realization of the humanity of *one* slave: Jim. (And it's important to note that Huck's change of heart applies only to Jim, not to the institution of slavery or any other person of Jim's race.) Epiphanies— flashes of insight—may appear to happen suddenly, but if you look more carefully at the events in the story and how characters react to them, you can trace pivotal revelations back to smaller moments that affect the character, leading slowly but surely to a character's major internal change. That is why it is important for readers to understand the significance of every event in the story and to pair it with the main character's reaction.

One way of grappling with Reading Standard 3 is by teaching students to perceive a character's "worldview," by which we mean the lens through which a character's world is colored. Let's take this abstract idea and bring it to the level of a simple story that lends itself to Reading Standard 3: *Horton Hatches the Egg* (Geiss, 1940). In case you have forgotten, this is a story of a helpful (but sadly naïve) elephant, Horton, who agrees to do an acquaintance (the despicable Mayzie the lazy bird) a favor by sitting on her egg while she abandons her responsibility by indulging in a little frivolity in Palm Beach. After Horton has endured a full year of eventful, dangerous, humiliating, not to mention uncomfortable egg-sitting, Mayzie, the thankless lazy bird, has the nerve to demand her well-sat-upon egg back as though a whole year of faithfulness on Horton's part means nothing. The reader can assume that, in the beginning of the story, when we first meet Horton, he had no idea how great an attachment he would develop for someone else's egg. We can say that, at the beginning, Horton viewed the world as a place where when someone asks you for a favor, you just do it, and you can be confident that all will go well. Horton's worldview in the beginning is that the world is fair place, a place where elephants and birds should help each other out when they can. Ah, but Horton's experiences change as the story progresses. It can be said that in the middle of the story, Horton views the world as a place fraught with dangers, everything from icy cold to taunting peers to, finally, elephant-nappers who would cage you and your helpless ward to be carted off to the circus. Ultimately, after Horton's egg hatches to release a baby elephant-bird hybrid, his view of the world resolves into one where justice prevails: "And it should be, it should be, it should be like that. Because Horton was faithful. He sat and he sat."

Those are the three worldviews of Horton, worldviews that are shaped by the events in the story. But every story is about a main character whose worldview undergoes changes. Being able to track and articulate those changes, tying them to events in the story, is what Reading Standard 3 (for literature) is about.

In *The Watsons Go to Birmingham—1963* (Christopher Paul Curtis, 1995), the main character is Kenny Watson. His worldview in the beginning of the story is that the world (Flint, Michigan) is a place ruled by his tough-acting, trouble-seeking, bullying older brother Byron. In the middle of the book, Kenny comes to see the world as a place where Byron is outmatched by their parents, who plan on delivering Byron to the tender mercies of their Southern grandmother, a woman who will know how to handle him and remove him from the urban dangers of Flint. But by the end of the book, after Kenny witnesses the infamous burning of a church in Birmingham where four little girls perished, he views the world as a place where evil runs far deeper, even "down home," than he could have imagined, and where Byron actually risked his own life to save him from drowning.

Most stories are about the reluctant journey: This is a paradigm where main characters find themselves yanked out of their comfort zone (home). To survive in a new environment, they need to call upon skills they didn't know they had. They are forced to re-evaluate themselves, others, and the world itself and what it's all about. They experience epiphanies. They change their worldviews, usually twice: The first change occurs as they adapt to their new environment, and then again by the story's resolution. The change in worldview is usually the result of a loss of innocence, a loss that results in wisdom and a deepening of values. It may be helpful to have students construct a graphic organizer, linking events and conversations to the corresponding characters. On the graphic organizer, leave room for the student to indicate the significance of these conversations and events, emphasizing how they affect the plot and/or theme.

A good source of practice for Reading Standard 3 may be found in Shakespearean soliloquies. *You don't have to teach the whole play!* Most of the soliloquies may be taught as stand-alones, provided that you give just a small amount of context. For Reading Standard 3, we are interested in the kind of soliloquy in which a character is having an out-loud argument with himself or herself before deciding on a course of action. Such arguments have definite progressions: the dilemma, the pros, the cons, the speculations, the resolution. When students can follow the arguments, when they can see the turning points, they are engaging in Reading Standard 3.

For example, here is Juliet, deciding whether or not to drink the death-simulating potion that Friar Lawrence has given to her, so that her parents will think she is dead on the day that she is supposed to marry Paris, freeing her to remain married to Romeo, who will come to wake her up and whisk her away. (And, no, it is not a good plan, as, leaving aside the grief Juliet is causing her parents, wouldn't she eventually have to wake up anyway and just have to marry Paris at that point? But, no one ever said Friar Lawrence dispensed good advice.) With some help with some of the language, students in the 6–8 grade band can track the progressions of Juliet's thoughts. (You will also have to explain to them that Tybalt is Juliet's cousin, whom Romeo recently killed in a street fight in retribution for Tybalt's having killed Romeo's friend Mercutio.)

Juliet:

> My dismal scene I needs must act alone.
> Come, vial.
> What if this mixture do not work at all?
> Shall I be married then tomorrow morning?
> No, no, this shall forbid it.
> Lie thou there. (*lays her knife down*)
> What if it be a poison, which the friar
> Subtly hath ministered to have me dead
> Lest in this marriage he should be dishonored
> Because he married me before to Romeo?
> I fear it is. And yet, methinks it should not,
> For he hath still been a tried and holy man.
> How, if when I am laid into the tomb,
> I wake before the time that Romeo
> Come to redeem me? There's a fearful point.
> Shall I not, then, be stifled in the vault
> To whose foul mouth no healthsome air breathes in,
> And there lie strangled ere my Romeo comes?
> Or, if I live, is it not very like
> The horrible conceit of death and night,
> Together with the terror of the place,
> As in a vault, an ancient receptacle,
> Where for these many hundred years the bones
> Of all my buried ancestors are packed;
> Where bloody Tybalt, yet but green in earth,
> Lies festering in his shroud, where, as they say,
> At some hour in the night spirits resort—?

Alack, alack, is it not like that I,
So early waking, with what loathsome smells,
And shrieks like mandrakes torn out of the earth,
That living mortals, hearing them, run mad—?
Or, if I wake, shall I not be distraught,
Environ-ed with all these hideous fears,
And madly play with my forefathers' joints,
And pluck the mangled Tybalt from his shroud,
And in this rage with some great kinsman's bone,
As with a club, dash out my desperate brains?
Oh, look, methinks I see my cousin's ghost
Seeking out Romeo, that did spit his body
Upon a rapier's point. Stay, Tybalt, Stay!
Romeo, Romeo, Romeo! Here's drink! I drink to thee!
Act IV, Scene iii, lines 19–58

Students will be meeting Reading Standard 3 as they discuss where the turning points are in this soliloquy, i.e., following Juliet's train of thought as she ultimately decides to drink the potion despite her misgivings. (Note that the last line—Juliet's decision to drink the potion—is unexpected, given that her fears are spiraling out of control. Ask students how, as a director, they would resolve this contradiction on the stage: How much of a pause would precede the last line? What would you have Juliet do during such a pause? How would Juliet say Romeo's name differently each of the three times she says it?)

While we're on the subject of Shakespeare, whose works are specifically promoted in the Common Core, we don't have to postpone these thrilling stories and their delicious language for high school. We can treat our students in the lower grades to morsels of the language through the picture book *Something Rich and Strange: A Treasury of Shakespeare Verse* (Gina Pollinger and Emma Chichester), and we can give them accessible versions of many of the stories through Charles and Mary Lamb's *Tales from Shakespeare*. Also, many of the plays have been made into graphic novels.

To summarize how Reading Standard 3 applies to literary text, in grades 3–8, students are learning how the literary elements of plot (events and conversations) and setting act upon the main character to advance the story, episode by episode. They are learning that events and conversations in the story may seem unimportant or even irrelevant, but that all of the story elements do serve a purpose, and that purpose is to affect (change the worldview) of the main character. Reading Standard 3 matches perfectly with Writing Standard 3: "Write narratives to develop real or imagined experiences or events using effective technique, well-chosen details, and well-structured event sequences."

Reading Standard 3 for Informational Text

> ## Tip
>
> Keep some perspective: Where have students been, prior to Grade 4?
>
> Grade 3: Informational: Describe the relationship between a series of historical events, scientific ideas or concepts, or steps in technical procedures in a text, using language that pertains to time, sequence, and cause/effect.
>
> Where are students expected to go, after Grade 8?
>
> Grades 9–10: Informational: Analyze how the author unfolds an analysis or series of ideas or events, including the order in which the points are made, how they are introduced and developed, and the connections that are drawn between them.

Reading Standard 3 is one of the standards in which the skills for literary text differ from those of informational text. Informational text does not have plot events and conversations that affect characters who are placed in a setting. Informational text elaborates upon a subject, which may be an individual, event, or idea. How do we instruct students to delineate the development of ideas in informational text? One way is to show students what it means to relate the details that the author chooses to give to the author's main idea (Reading Standard 2). The key questions are: *Why is this detail here?* or *What is the relationship between this detail and the paragraph in which it appears? What is the relationship between this paragraph and the section in which it appears? What is the relationship between this section and the whole piece?*

Is there an **anecdote**? If so, why is it there? Authors choose anecdotes because they illustrate a point. What point does a particular anecdote illustrate?

Are there **examples**? If so, what are they examples of?

Are there **embedded definitions**? Of what words or terms? Authors choose to include definitions for one of two reasons: Either the author is using a term that most readers do not know, or, the author is creating a limited definition (called a "working definition") for the purpose of this particular discussion.

Are there **detailed descriptions** that you can visualize? If so, why has the author included them?

Are there **explanations**? Explanations usually include statements of cause and effect. Explanations usually answer the question *Why?* We usually see words like *cause, because, effect, affect, reason/s, results, therefore, since,* and *so* structuring an explanation. We often see phrases like *that is why, leading to, what happens is,* and pairs like *if . . . then.*

Are there **sequences**? Sequences lay events out in time order. This may mean that one event depends on the next, or it may just be that the events are being told in the order in which they occurred, without a causal connection. Procedures are presented as sequences.

Are there **comparisons**? Comparisons emphasize similarities. What two things are being compared? What are the similarities between them that have caused the author to compare them?

Are there **contrasts**? Contrasts emphasize differences. What two things are being contrasted? What are the differences between them that have caused the author to contrast them?

Is a **system** being described? The purpose of informational text is often to explain a system of interdependent components, or a system of classification (called a *taxonomy*) where items fall into categories that are further divided into sub-categories.

Standard 3 Summary

Think of informational text as having ingredients like the ingredients of a lunch box. The meat (or other protein) of the sandwich is the main idea (Reading Standard 2: Main idea), which is held together by the bread (Language Standards 4, 5: Vocabulary acquisition and use) and the other components, as delineated above, are the optional side dishes (Reading Standard 3: Understand and follow progressions, seeing how the details support the main idea) that go together with the sandwich. The well-packed lunch box would include a beverage, and that would be the overall organizational structure (Reading Standard 5: Organizational structure), as well as some condiments (Reading Standard 6: Point of view) and utensils (Reading Standard 4: Understanding how the words are used in context).

Guiding Questions for Readers: Standard 3

1. (Literary Text): What is the relationship between any two literary elements? (How do these elements affect each other?) This is *not* a comparison/contrast question. This is a synthesis question, where we are asking students to synthesize any two literary elements in terms of the story as a whole, for example: characters and setting; plot and theme; characters and theme, narrative point of view and characters.

2. (Informational Text): What is the connection between any of the two "ingredients" of the text? This is also a synthesis question, where we are asking the students to synthesize any two elements of informational text in terms of the whole message, for example: anecdote and explanation; detailed description and embedded definition; examples and explanation, etc.

7 Reading Standards 4–6
Craft and Structure

Standards 4–6 focus on the question: Why did the author choose to make particular choices? How do choices about language, organization, and point of view affect meaning? Many teachers have not delved into these features of text, and may find that the considerations inherent in these Reading Standards do take comprehension to an unexplored level.

In this chapter:

Reading Standard 4: Figure Out the Meaning of Words and Phrases

Reading Standard 4: Interpret words and phrases as they are used in a text, including determining technical, connotative, and figurative meanings, and analyze how specific word choices shape meaning or tone. (www.corestandards. org/ELA-Literacy/CCRA/R/4)

Tip

Keep some perspective: Where have students been, prior to Grade 4?

Grade 3: Literary: Determine the meaning of words and phrases as they are used in a text, distinguishing literal from nonliteral language.

Informational: Determine the meaning of general academic and domain-specific words and phrases in a text relevant to a Grade 3 topic or subject area.

Where are students expected to go, after Grade 8?

Grades 9–10:

Literary: Determine the meaning of words and phrases as they are used in a text, including figurative and connotative meanings; analyze the cumulative impact of specific word choices on meaning and tone (e.g., how the language evokes a sense of time and place; how it sets a formal or informal tone).

The Reading Standard for informational text is the same as for literary text.

Reading Standard 4 is about vocabulary skills, which include not only knowing definitions but, moreover, understanding the author's intention and attitude through diction (word choice). *Why is one word used rather than another word with a similar meaning? Is there a running theme among the words? How is figurative language used? How is technical language used?*

No one questions the foundational role that vocabulary plays in comprehension. The rule of thumb is that a reader needs to know at least 90% of the words in a text for it to be at the reader's instructional level. (A reader who knows fewer than that percentage is reading at his frustration level.) Because of its importance, vocabulary skills appear explicitly in two of the Language Standards, in addition to Reading Standard 4.

> Language Standard 4: Determine or clarify the meaning of unknown and multiple-meaning words and phrases by using context clues, analyzing meaningful word parts, and consulting general and specialized reference materials, as appropriate.
>
> Language Standard 5: Demonstrate understanding of figurative language, word relationships, and nuances in word meanings. (www. corestandards.org)

In addition to Language Standards 4 and 5, when we're talking about close reading (Reading Standard 1) and certainly when we're talking about any of the Writing Standards, vocabulary learning plays a tremendous role.

Consider that Reading Standard 4 is placed within the "Craft and Structure" grouping (rather than with Reading Standards 1–3, which are grouped as "Key Ideas and Details"). To meet Standard 4, readers have to know more about the words in the text than just their definitions. Words are like people: They have relatives (Latin and Greek affixes and roots), they play different roles (adapting into different parts of speech to fit into a sentence), and they have etymologies ("back stories") that help us understand them on a deeper level. And words have attitudes. We call a word's attitude its connotation, the emotional freight that a word carries aside from its denotation (dictionary definition). The collective effect of the connotation of key words in a text creates its tone. Tone is a property of writers' craft.

As you can see, Reading Standard 4 is one of the Standards that does not differ significantly from one grade to another. Although students are expected to recognize allusions beginning in Grade 4, the ability to do so permeates all of the grades, becoming more demanding as they read texts that assume recognition of more (and less familiar) allusions. Figurative language, connotation, and technical language are also important throughout the grade levels: It isn't that we're really adding any of these from one grade level to another. We are, perhaps, refining the terminology and expecting that students can draw from a greater storehouse of literary techniques and the Greek affixes that are the hallmark of technical language.

Reading Standard 4 for Literary Text

We'll categorize the language demands for Reading Standard 4 in literary text into allusions, tropes, connotation, and motifs. We'll be talking about how to infuse these features of literary language at all of the grade levels at once as an integral part of how we teach literature.

Allusions: Let's start with allusions, if only because they are specifically mentioned for fourth grade. Everyone recognizes allusions automatically, provided that they know the original source. A first grader will recognize an allusion to Batman, Superman, Barbie, or the Wicked Witch of the West *if* she knows the stories. She won't, of course, know the word *allusion.* The word itself is the noun form of *allude* (*to make a disguised reference to*). Why disguise a reference? Why not just make a direct reference? The root of allude is *–lude,* meaning *to play.* Accordingly, it is a relative of *prelude, interlude, illusion, delude/delusion, collude/collusion,* even *ludicrous.* See the connection?

If you try to teach the word *allusion* directly, most students will not understand it through a definition alone: *An allusion is an incidental reference . . .* You've lost them. The concept is learned not through definition but through numerous examples identified with known language: *"refers to . . .," "gets you to remember . . ."* You can teach the word *allusion* (*allude* to) indirectly just by using it repeatedly to point out examples. (But your students will confuse it with *illusion* unless you point it out in written form many times, explaining the difference.)

Perhaps the most accessible allusions to elementary children are found in names of pet dogs and cats. It's easier to teach the concept of allusion through a cat named Cleo or Nala (named for people other than cats) than through names of fictitious cats (Felix, Sylvester.) The best allusions are more than just namesakes. They are more like doors which lead to deeper truths.

To understand allusions, elementary children can investigate names of sports teams: What is it about the name of a team that evokes a quality that the team wants to adopt, or an admired feature about the history or geography of the team's location.

You'll notice that many of the Reading Standards call for the reading of fairy tales, folktales from various cultures, Greek and Roman mythology, and the Bible stories. Aside from their inherent value, these sources are constantly alluded to in other literature. An allusion is like a hyperlink on the Internet: A mental click on it enriches meaning. The Reading Standards have us broadening that base of cultural literacy that enables students to recognize that the hyperlink/allusion is there.

The inability to recognize an allusion is arguably more detrimental to comprehension than a word whose meaning is unknown to the reader. This is because the reader knows she doesn't know the unfamiliar word. She might actively seek out the meaning of an unfamiliar word using the usual tools of word analysis, context, or outside assistance. But a missed allusion is a missed opportunity for deeper meaning not just of a single word but of a concept that the author clearly wanted the reader to grasp. And if you miss an allusion, you don't even know that you've missed it.

But all the teaching in the world *about* allusions will not help readers recognize them. Only background knowledge gleaned from exposure to cultural touchstones in the arts and history, and the world in general will do that. A significant difference still exists between middle-class and impoverished children regarding exposure to stories and background knowledge. ". . . great disparities exist among middle- and low-income communities in resources available in homes or child-care sites. . . . 60% of the kindergartners in neighborhoods where children did poorly in school did not own a single book. Given the estimate that a typical middle-class child enters first grade with approximately 1,000 hours of being read to, while the corresponding child from a low-income family averages just 25 hours, such differences in the availability of book resources may have unintended and pernicious consequences for low-income children's long-term success in schooling" (Newman, 1990) Although that quotation comes from an article written in 1990 (*Reading Research Quarterly*), the statistics remain grim, with 61% of children from low-income families having no books at all in the home accessible to children (http://teacher.scholastic.com/products/face-new/about.html#access-to-books).

When children come to our classes lacking the exposure to traditional literature, one way we can make up for the gaps is to have reading stations where groups of students read different fairy tales, folktales, and myths and then explain them to the class. This is an efficient way to differentiate instruction while increasing everybody's knowledge base. Because allusions refer to famous elements of stories, not to details, having a general idea about various stories is helpful.

Tropes: Trope is a catch-all term for widely-understood metaphors, similes, puns, figures of speech, memes, and paradigms. Authors use tropes to enrich meaning by creating a kind of layered reality in which one word, image or model signifies more than one thing. Common story tropes are the fish-out-of-water situation, the neighborhood-bogeyman-saves-the-day, the underdog story, and the ugly-duckling scenario. Broadly, a trope is any recognizable symbol, pattern, or archetype that helps us understand something in a larger context, or in addition to its literal meaning. (For example, in the story of the Tortoise and the Hare, we understand that the meaning of the story is larger than two particular animals having a race. And when we read *Hamlet*, we understand that its meaning is larger than one particular Prince and his difficulties in adjusting to a new family situation.)

Reading Standard 4 calls for discussions of metaphor and simile as tropes in the fifth grade, but figurative language has been introduced in third grade, if not before. In fifth grade, students need to answer questions about what is literal and what is metaphorical. The difference between a metaphor and a simile is straightforward because a simile explicitly uses the words *like* or *as* to establish a comparison. However, the job is not done when students can recognize this distinction. The more important concept is that students in the fifth grade understand not only what is literal and what is figurative, but also the effect of the trope, such as a metaphor. We can start by asking if the association created by the metaphor is intended to be positive or negative. That broad difference is usually clear. From there, we may be able to narrow it down.

For example, one of the poems in the Grade 4–5 band is the sonnet "The New Colossus" by Emma Lazarus, written in 1883 to honor the Statue of Liberty. The title and first line of the poem allude to the Colossus of Rhodes (an allusion which needs to be explained, obviously) and then employs several metaphors regarding light. Although Lady Liberty holds high a literal lamp, light is still a metaphor in this poem, representing such positive concepts as welcome, hope, finding one's way, and newness. Light is a trope that often represents intelligence, but in this poem there is no evidence to suggest that interpretation. The teachable points of Reading Standard 4 are that 1) a Colossus means two things, which are the same in their grandeur, but different in their functions; 2) the many references to lights (torch, flame, lightning, beacon, lamp, golden door) are there to evoke certain ideas that fit into the poem, and not others that might mean something else in a different context; and 3) although some of the references to light are literal (torch, flame, beacon, lamp), they are also metaphorical. We know this because they represent something larger than themselves: Lady Liberty is not holding a lamp just to lead ships to the New York harbor. There would have been simpler ways to accomplish that. She is holding an actual (literal) lamp because of the ideas that a lamp represents.

Connotation: Grade 6 brings us in to connotation, the emotional triggers of certain words. Not all words are connotative. People differ in their responses to words: One person's *casual* is another's *careless, lazy, neglectful,* or *sloppy* just as one person's *formal* is another's *snooty, snobby, overdressed, stiff,* or *ostentatious.* Is a movie *violent* or is it *action-packed*? Is a child in your class *bratty* or is he *high-spirited*? That the same observable phenomenon takes on a different reality depending on the connotation of the word we choose to describe it is the subject of much philosophy. But how do we teach connotation to sixth graders?

If there's one thing sixth graders know, probably better than we do, it is lyrics to popular music. Lyrics are highly connotative. By asking students to consider word choice in relation to meaning in a rap or song, you can get them talking about connotative meanings (which are highly contextual).

Language found in everyday life, such as menus and advertising, are rich sources of connotative language. Once students can recognize words with distinctly positive and negative connotations, they can understand how an author intends for them to regard characters and settings: Is the character *smiling* or *smirking*? Is the house *rustic* or is it *crude*? Be careful, though, to stay within the same concept when expressing a spectrum of words having different connotations: The difference between "she *barged* in" and "she *burst* in" is a matter of connotation; the difference between "she *barged* in" and "she *crept* in" is a difference in the actual denotation of the two words.

Motifs: When several words or words representing the same concept are repeated, we call that a motif. Motifs are not accidental; they convey the author's intent. In The Gettysburg Address, Lincoln uses the word *dedicate* six times, along with the closely related word *devotion* (used twice) and *consecrate* (used twice). These words, having a religious connotation, play a large role in establishing the tone of somber contemplation for the occasion.

Motifs do not hide. Begin by asking students simply to notice what words are repeated. If no words are repeated, ask them to notice what words go together. Motifs can also be expressed through contrast. Ask students to find words within a passage that are opposites. How do these opposites set against each other to convey the author's meaning?

Tip

A great way to discover motifs is by creating a "word cloud" through an Internet tool called Wordle (www.wordle.net).

Sound and Sense

The effect of poetry is derived from sounds of the words as well as their meaning. Emphasis is achieved through rhythm, rhyme, refrain, alliteration, onomatopoeia, and a whole variety of rhetorical devices involving different kinds of repetition. According to Reading Standard 4, seventh graders should be learning about the aural features of literature. It is not necessary to go into more detail than to teach examples of a few basic terms, such as those listed above, and have students understand that their purpose is usually to draw the reader's attention to the meaning by creating special sounds. Rhythm, rhyme, and refrain create an organizational pattern that facilitates memorization and that imparts a sense of completion as well as "specialness" of the literature.

The rhyme can be sing-song, such as in "Casey at the Bat," which gives that poem the feel of a child-like story. But one of the most difficult concepts to get across to middle school students is that poems do not necessarily have to rhyme. They will say, "Well, if it doesn't rhyme, then why is it a poem?" Not a bad question. Seventh graders may be ready to learn that poetry is poetry and not prose because . . . well, because the person who wrote it decided to call it a poem and have it look like a poem. However, when we look and listen to the poem carefully, we will find that even though it does not rhyme, poetry uses the sounds of words in special ways to enhance the meaning of the words. There may be near-rhyme (Emily Dickenson), alliteration (Poe), onomatopoeia (Poe), and all kinds of obvious and subtle kinds of repetition and even wordplay. Seventh graders are ready to be invited into poetry to discover sound-based devices other than sing-song rhyme.

Reading Standard 4 for literary text needs to be more than an exercise in memorizing rhetorical terms and picking out examples. Students need to connect the terms to actual meaning in the literature. Rhetorical devices and figurative language illuminate meaning, and that is the value of naming them.

Informational Text: Reading Standard 4

Informational text that uses rhetorical devices and figurative language is called literary nonfiction. Students in grades 6 and beyond are expected to be reading literary nonfiction as well as unembellished informational text, which we can call technical language.

Technical language is purely functional: textbooks, instructional manuals, contracts and other legal documents, math problems, reports, reference books. Technical words are highly specific. They don't have synonyms, so they are likely to be repeated within a text, but not for poetic purposes, such as emphasis or rhythm. Technical language is always straight-forward, never ironic.

Technical words tend to be polysyllabic, but the good news is that, because of that, they have components (prefixes, roots, affixes) that allow us to break them down into known parts and derive meaning by associating them with other words of a similar structure. It is very helpful to make cross-disciplinary links between technical words. For example, the word *technical* is related to *technique, technology,* and *technician.* The secret is in the Greek components, but you can't just give out a list of those and have students memorize them. Greek components appear again and again in technical language, and students will learn them as they see these connections. Seeing connections among words that share a structural ancestry leads to durable and deep understanding of words.

Technical language is "insider" language, and its very use (or lack thereof) marks the speaker/reader as an insider or outsider. Whether the field is plumbing, nursing, photography, or neurosurgery, professionals use professional language. Initiation of the novice into the professional conversation is a large part of the job of teachers and role models. But a feature of language is that we sometimes understand words aurally but not visually, having heard a word but not read it. Because of their Greek pedigree, technical words are spelled with combinations of letters that are not often seen in ordinary words: *ps, ph, phy, ch*-(k), *ae, oe, x*, and endings -*sis*, -*yze*, -*ium* to name a few. The length of technical words can also interfere with mental pronunciations, which are important to comprehension. Poor readers tend to confuse words that have the same beginnings, disregarding everything after the first one or two syllables. Thus, technical words like *geocentric, geothermal*, and *geographic* might be mistaken for each other.

Technical words, because of their specificity, can usually be presented as pictures. Many technical words name processes and structures which are already illustrated in diagrams in the text.

One more feature about technical language is that phrases function as single units of meaning more than phrases do in literary language. In social studies, we have phrases like *branches of government, Bill of Rights, civil rights movement*, and countless others. In science, we have *chemical reaction, atomic weight, soil erosion, electromagnetic radiation*. In math, there are even more. The significance of this is that readers need to process such phrases as phrases not as single words being seen for the first time. We need to keep this condition of technical language in mind as we teach readers in the content areas.

Standard 4 Summary

Reading Standard 4 for literary text is about the effects—not just the name—of word choices, including figurative language, and about rhetorical devices on meaning, leading us to ask: *Why did the author choose this particular word?* The same question can be asked of diction (word choice) in literary nonfiction. For purely informational text, we're looking at technical language. Technical words tend to be multi-syllabic, Greek-based (and therefore connected to other technical words), specific, and capable of being presented in a visual form. Also, phrases in technical language often function as single words.

Guiding Questions for Readers: Standard 4

1. For literary text: Why did the author choose a particular word or phrase, when there were two or more other possibilities available in the English language? Does the author's choice of a word or phrase have a particular connotation that makes sense in the story, drama, or poem? In a poem, does a particular word have sound qualities (rhythm, alliteration) that make it fit in?

2. For informational text: What are the components (prefix, root, suffix) of a particular technical word? What other technical words are related to it?

Reading Standard 5: Text Structure

Reading Standard 5: Analyze the structure of texts, including how specific sentences, paragraphs, and larger portions of the text (e.g., a section, chapter, scene, or stanza) relate to each other and the whole. (www.corestandards.org/ELA-Literacy/CCRA/R/5)

Reading Standard 5 is about understanding how and why the author decided to arrange the story or information in a particular way. To answer questions about Reading Standard 5, we need to take a bird's eye view of the text, considering it as a whole.

Let's talk about the word *structure*. Although we use this word in school a lot, it represents an abstract concept, and many students will not understand how to apply it to text. (Like the words *function*, and *value*, the word *structure* is used throughout the student's day, with its meaning varying from one subject to another. The structure of a story is intangible, unlike the structure of a building, plant cell, battery, or even a mathematical equation. Parts of a story flow into each other. Chapter names, if they exist, capture the content of each chapter, not the elements of the structure of the story as a whole: Chapters are not named *exposition, rising action, climax, falling action, denouement.* We scaffold students' understanding of story structure by naming the parts and using a graphic organizer called Freytag's Pyramid.

Developed by the German novelist Gustov Freytag in the 19th century, the pyramid delineates the six developmental stages of a story: exposition, inciting incident, rising action, climax, falling action (aka resolution), denouement (aka ending). The Freytag model is a variation on Aristotle's three-act dramatic structure, and both of these models remain a good way to concretize what we mean by "structure" in a story.

Note

Standard 5 connects to the next Standard, Standard 6, which asks us to consider point of view: Is there a single narrator? Some stories have multiple narrators. Sometimes, each narrator will tell part of the story; more rarely, but interestingly, various narrators will give their perspectives on the same event.

In the structure of stories, plotlines converge and intertwine to create a theme (Reading Standard 2), characters grow (Reading Standard 3), the meaning of seemingly tangential details emerge (Reading Standard 1), and the satisfied reader sees just how the story is a unified whole (Reading Standard 5).

Tip

Keep some perspective: Where have students been, prior to Grade 4?

Grade 3: Literary: Refer to parts of stories, dramas, and poems when writing or speaking about a text, using terms such as chapter, scene, and stanza; describe how each successive part builds on earlier sections. (www.corestandards.org/ELA-Literacy/RL/3)

Informational: Use text features and search tools (e.g., key words, sidebars, hyperlinks) to locate information relevant to a given topic efficiently. (www.corestandards.org/ELA-Literacy/RI/3)

Where are the students expected to go, after Grade 8?

Grades 9–10: Literary: Analyze how an author's choices concerning how to structure a text, order events within it (e.g., parallel plots), and manipulate time (e.g., pacing, flashbacks) create such effects as mystery, tension, or surprise. (www.corestandards.org/ELA-Literacy/RL/9–10)

Informational: (www.corestandards.org/ELA-Literacy/RI/3)
Where have students been, prior to Grade 4?

Reading Standard 5 for Literary Text: Grade by Grade

Beginning in Grade 4, students are building a storehouse of vocabulary about literary structure and genre. They already know words like *poetry, poem, story,* and *play* and can identify these genres on the basis of their appearance. Although fourth graders intuitively know how to use these terms, now is the time to give them more precise, domain-specific definitions.

Doing so is a little tricky: *Story,* after all, is a word that can refer to an anecdote within informational text, a novel, a movie, a memoir, a play, a narrative poem. For the purpose of Reading Standard 5, let's use the word *story* to refer to a prose work (more on that term in the next paragraph). For fourth graders, chapter books (aka novels) and short stories may be called "stories." *Drama* broadly refers to any kind of conflict or emotional outburst. But when it comes to Reading Standard 5, we'll use the word *drama* to refer to scripts. To qualify as drama, a work of literature must be laid out as a dialogue, with some stage directions, a list of characters, and perhaps a description of the setting. While it is true that all literature is driven by the drama within it, we'll be establishing the difference between a dramatic scene in a chapter book and *drama* as its own genre. Finally, poetry: Narrative poems, such as "Casey at the Bat," are stories. Stories in narrative poems contain drama. To sum up: In fourth grade, Reading Standard 5 directs us to agree on genre-based applications of the words *story*, *drama*, and *poetry*. We will also be using story and drama less formally, as we speak of the story that is told by a play or poem, and the drama that exists within those stories. Sorry, but that's just the nature of the language that we use to speak about literature.

Fortunately, it's pretty easy to recognize these three broad genres: Stories look like stories. Dramas look like scripts. Poetry looks like poetry. The appearance—the layout—of literature on the page is a legitimate, if basic, structural feature. Now would be the time to start using the word *prose*. Many people mistakenly use the word *prose* to mean *poetry*, and I'm guessing that's because the word *prose* is often used in conversations about poetry, and there's something about the word that, ironically, evokes poetry. But let's get this straight: Prose connotes literature (or any written text) that is *not* poetry. If writing on a page looks like poetry, it is poetry. If it looks like ordinary language, it is prose. And, yes, a writer can, if he or she so chooses, take prose, lay it out on the page so that it looks like poetry, and call it poetry. However, we hope poets are not doing that, and we certainly want to define poetry for students such that poetry means more to them than "words on a page arranged to look like poetry" even though that broad definition is technically accurate.

So, if poetry is merely words on a page that are arranged to look like poetry, what else can be said about poetry? Well, poetry not only looks like poetry, it also sounds like poetry. That is not to say that all poems rhyme. But all poems have a deliberate rhythm, a beat, that the poet has arranged.

As for drama, let's just define that for fourth graders as literature that turns into a play when you read it aloud with others. Technically speaking, drama is a type of prose

Therefore, fourth grade is a good time to introduce the word *genre*, meaning, simply "kind of," to differentiate the three broad types of literature: prose (literature that is not poetry or drama), poetry (with apologies for the circular definition: literature that is arranged on the page to look like a poem, so that when you read it aloud, it sounds like a poem), and drama (literature that is arranged on the page like a conversation, with a few stage directions).

Beginning in Grade 5, students learn how to "explain how a series of chapters, scenes, or stanzas fits together to provide the overall structure of the particular story, drama, or poem." To accomplish this Reading Standard, fifth graders need to understand what is meant by the "overall structure" of a work of literature. Remember that "overall structure" does not mean "overall meaning," which would be Standard 2 (central theme).

"Overall structure" has to do with the arrangement of the events in a story, drama, or narrative poem; or the arrangement of the descriptions in a lyric poem. (A narrative poem tells a story; a lyric poem expresses a feeling and/or describes a scene.)

Authors give us groupings: chapters, scenes, stanzas. Each of the units contributes to what happens next, and to the overall story arc and themes. The essential questions that Reading Standard 5 asks at the fifth grade level are:

1. Why is this chapter (scene, stanza) included? How would the story be different if this chapter (scene, stanza) were left out?

2. Which of the literary elements does this chapter (story, scene) focus on most? If it is mostly action, with important events moving the story along, we can say that it focuses on plot. If it is mostly description of a place at a particular time, we can say that it focuses on setting. If it is mostly about the thoughts, feelings, and reasoning of a character, then we can say that it focuses on character. If it is mostly philosophical, then we can say that it focuses on theme.

To engage fifth graders in Reading Standard 5, we can give them story events in scrambled order and have them put them back together, justifying the order in which they, and the author, arrange them. This activity can be done on an interactive white board, or with index cards, with students themselves holding cards with chapter (scene, stanza) summarizing statements or key quotations and arranging themselves to recapitulate the story.

Some sentence frames for expressing understanding of Reading Standard 5 at the fifth grade level are: This chapter (scene, stanza) . . .

1. . . . helps me to *understand* _____ because . . .

2. . . . helps me to *visualize* _____ because . . .

3. . . . is included in the story because . . .

4. . . . cannot be in another part of the story because . . .

Then in the sixth grade, students dig deeper into Reading Standard 5, as they move from whole chapters (scenes, stanzas) into single sentences, quotations, and close-ups, analyzing the significance of these details. But the questions, activities, and sentence frames described above still apply, just on a more granular level.

In the seventh grade, students begin to consider some of the sub-categories within the three major genres (prose stories, drama, poetry). It is now that they will be breaking down prose stories into such subgenres as:

The Detective Story: In the classic "whodunit," a detective—professional, amateur, or unwitting—is tasked with solving a mystery by inferring information from clues. Plot devices that are the usual suspects in this subgenre are the misleading clues (red herrings), seemingly trivial details that turn out to be important in solving the mystery (real clues), a detective and a foil to the detective (a character whose purpose is to allow the detective to explain his or her methods of interpreting the clues). The parts of the detective story are the crime, the clues, character and setting descriptions, the resolution.

The Quest: Also called "The Hero's Journey," this format begins with a character who feels a vague sense of dissatisfaction, a mild itch for adventure, or an outright sense of not belonging in his or her environment. The character is then pitched into another world and, with a little help from a fairy godmother and a lot of harm from wicked witches, the character realizes undiscovered strength. The quest ends with the character returning home, with newly-found deep appreciation, but an abiding sense of alienation. Any "road trip" story follows this model.

The Unexpected Price: This format, also called the Faustian bargain, is quite common, especially in myths and fairy tales ("The Fisherman and his Wife," "The Little Mermaid," "The Sorcerer's Apprentice"). In it, a person achieves his or her greatest desire but ends up sacrificing something much more valuable, a sacrifice that he or she did not foresee.

The Reversal: In this structure, the tables are turned on the expected story line. For example, in O. Henry's "The Ransom of Red Chief" the kidnappers end up paying to return their bratty hostage to the father, who was in no hurry to be reunited with his rambunctious child. In Roald Dahl's *Matilda*, Matilda's parents are rash and foolish while she is wise and mature. Often, reversals are due to hubris—the Greek-inspired word for excessive pride—in which a character subverts his or her own success by believing in his or her own invincibility. In that sense, the reversal pattern is similar to the Faustian bargain.

Romance: Love stories often are based on the pattern of having two people compelled toward each other despite the inconvenient, often fatal, enmity between their respective clans. Love stories thrive on irony, impossibility, disobedience, loss, violence, misunderstandings, and interference. The more disparate and incompatible the lovers appear on the surface, the better the story.

Subgenres are often born of the story models in Greek mythology, which should form a staple in middle school reading lists. Not only are its monsters, adventures, temptations, troubles, punishments, and excesses interesting to middle school students, but Greek mythology sets the stage for the expectations of Reading Standard 5 in eighth grade.

In eighth grade, Reading Standards 5 and 9 coincide: It is here that students: "Compare and contrast the structure of two or more texts and analyze how the differing structure of each text contributes to its meaning and style." If students come to eighth grade having read and analyzed the structure of a variety of Greek myths, they will be in position to compare how these myths are put together with traditional tales of Asia, Africa, native America, and the Bible.

Teaching Reading Standard 5 for Informational Text

Tip

Keep some perspective: Where are the students going in grades 9–10?

Analyze in detail how an author's ideas or claims are developed and refined by particular sentences, paragraphs, or larger portions of a text (e.g., sections or chapters. (www.corestandards.org/ELA-Literacy/RI/9–10)

Teaching Reading Standard 5 for Informational Text: Identifying Structure

Whereas Reading Standard 5 for literary text is about distinguishing features of genres and subgenres (story types), Reading Standard 5 for informational text is about how the main ideas and details are arranged. The rationale for Reading Standard 5, as it applies to informational text, is that readers are better able to comprehend relationships within the text and the meaning as a whole when they understand the overall organizational pattern. Think of a spacious, well-designed customized closet. It has lots of racks, shelves, hooks, compartments, pull-downs, hide-aways. Its design makes it efficient, so efficient that you don't even have to think much about it after it's been installed. It serves *you*. You don't have to paw through it, shoving aside extraneous items. Well-organized text is like that complex yet elegant closet, where form follows function. Reading Standard 5 for informational text is about the reader taking full advantage of the way in which the author has organized the text so that you can find what you need efficiently.

According to the language of the Common Core, students in fourth grade are expected to start building a vocabulary of text structures, i.e., ways in which information can be organized (arranged). Some of the terms needed to identify text structures are accessible, others are more abstract. It may be relatively easy for students to recognize that biographies, histories, and procedures are arranged in time (chronological) order, although the word *chronological* will be a mouthful for them. (It's one of those "difficult" words where the actual meaning is known but the sound and structure of the word itself makes it daunting and hard to remember.) Comparison/contrast structures and spatial structures (such as in a description of a place) may be relatively easy to recognize, but some of the others—cause and effect, problem and solution, classification, definition-example—require abstract thinking that will need significant scaffolding.

The best kind of scaffolding for Reading Standard 5 for informational text will be graphic organizers. Decide which kind of graphic organizer fits the text (T charts and Venn diagrams for comparison/contrast; timelines, Freytag Pyramids, and flowcharts for biographies, histories, and procedures; matrices and tree diagrams for classification; pro and con charts for argumentation; if/then flow charts for cause and effect chains). It's important that the right kind of graphic organizer is given to students to match the organizational pattern in whatever text they are reading. As students develop their skills in Reading Standard 5, they should be able to create their own graphic organizers, selecting the most appropriate forms.

It should be noted that authors don't necessarily commit to a single organizational pattern and then stick to it throughout their texts. Authors may have a predominant pattern—let's say it's classification, to explain life forms on the Great Barrier Reef. Within that overall pattern of classification, the author might branch off into cause and effect in a paragraph explaining why a particular organism lives in a particular place. The author may then devote a paragraph to the definition of a symbiotic relationship, supporting it with examples. But remember the closet metaphor: The overall purpose of the closet is to store a person's clothing, but the closet may also have nooks and crannies for particular accessories.

A typical reading comprehension text question that draws from Reading Standard 5 asks why a particular section (or paragraph or sentence) is included, or even why it is placed where it is. This kind of question requires the test-taker to perceive relationships and functions within an overall structure in which a given detail plays a part. Expect to see question stems like this:

The first (second, third . . .) paragraph serves the author's purpose by:

a. providing background information about _____
b. contrasting _____ with _____
c. establishing that the author is an expert in _____
d. giving an example of _____

The last sentence in paragraph 4 is included because it

a. gives an example of _____
b. explains the importance of _____
c. leads into paragraph 5
d. helps the reader visualize _____

Note these common organizational patterns:

- **Social studies and science textbooks** rely on paragraphs that begin with explicit topic sentences, followed by details. Reading Standard 5 is about having readers notice this pattern, and use it to assist them in making meaning by attaching the details within the paragraph to its first sentence, the topic sentence. The topic (first) sentence lays out a generality that is detailed in the sentences that follow in that paragraph. Some teachers like to have students turn the topic sentence into a question, a question that will be answered by the remainder of the paragraph.

- **Newspaper articles** are famous for following a particular organization structure of beginning with the 5W's (who, what, when, where, why) and then giving the information of the story in descending order of importance. This pattern helps busy readers move around the newspaper efficiently.

- **Information in a science textbook** is often arranged so as to allow the reader to visualize what something looks like. This is because much of the information in a science textbook is describing something that is either too small, too large, or too exotic for the reader to have actually seen. Therefore, much of the information in the science textbook is arranged spatially. Other favorite organizational patterns in science readings are cause and effect and classification.

Standard 5 Summary

Reading Standard 5 helps readers see the text as a whole, but, moreover, it helps them understand how structure *supports* meaning. To get to this point, graphic organizers, including outlines for informational text and the Freytag Pyramid for stories, are appropriate. But what students need to see is that recognizing, naming, and mapping the structure of a text is actually a strategy for accessing and recalling meaning. Furthermore, as students understand how structure operates for them as readers, they will be able to convert that understanding into becoming writers who produce organized structures.

Guiding Questions for Readers: Standard 5

1. For literary text: How does this story, drama, or narrative poem fit into the Freytag Pyramid?

2. For informational text: What kind of graphic organizer would best express the information? (Outline? Venn diagram? T-chart? matrix? flow chart?)

Reading Standard 6: Point of View

Reading Standard 6: Determine an author's point of view or purpose in a text and analyze how an author uses rhetoric to advance that point of view or purpose. (www.corestandards.org/ELA-Literacy/CCRA/R/6)

Reading Standard 6 is about understanding how an author establishes point of view, and that it is the reader's job to filter meaning *through* that point of view. The reader comes to understand not just the words and events, but how the author intends for the reader to interpret the words and events in light of the point of view that the author has chosen. Coming into the fourth grade, the students will have been exposed to the concept of point of view in terms of how their own point of view differs from that of the author: *"I think **this**. The character thinks **that**. I see **this**. The character sees **that**. I know **this**. The character knows **that**, etc."*

In the upper elementary school grades (4, 5, 6), Reading Standard 6, we're concerned mostly with developing an awareness of point of view, and a basic vocabulary about it. Here is what the progression looks like for literary text:

The first term that students in this grade band need is *narrator*, defined, simply, as "the person who is telling us the story." Because students (and sometimes, unfortunately, adults, even teachers) are in the habit of referring to the narrator as "they," rather than "the narrator," or "the author," we need to use the correct term frequently and consistently. That is a very simple practice that makes a big difference in understanding the concept of point of view, in using formal terminology in school (Language Standards 3 and 6: Both of which are about having the ability to adapt one's level of formality to the circumstances of communication), and in respecting both the author and the traditions of literature. (After all, an educated person does not say of the *Mona Lisa*: "I like how they did the background.")

After we've broken ourselves of the habit of referring to the narrator as anything other than "the narrator" (for literature) or "the author" (for informational text, or for literature when the author is the narrator), we need to teach fourth graders what the terms *first person, second person,* and *third person* mean, in regard to how we speak about narratives. You'll note that very few works of literature or even informational text (except for directions to the reader) are actually written in the second person. However, we can't just use the terms *first person* and *third person* without explaining who the second person is. So now would be the time to introduce pronouns, if the students don't know them already. (Speaking and Listening Standard 6; Language Standard 1: Both of these Standards relate to pronoun use indirectly, in terms of pronoun-antecedent agreement and formal use of pronoun case.)

Tip

The Real Truth About Pronouns: As everybody can recite, "a pronoun is a word that takes the place of a noun." However, that is not exactly true. If it were a sentence like "The little dog laughed and the dish ran away with the spoon," when the nouns were replaced by pronouns, would sound like this: "The little he laughed and the it ran away with the it." So, as you can see, what a pronoun really does it to take the place of a noun *and all of its modifiers.* Consider: "What annoys the actors most is when audience members think that turning down the volume on their cell phone ringers is the same as turning their phones off completely. It isn't." In this context, the pronoun *it* certainly does not take the place of any single noun. *It* stands in for the entire noun clause, which takes in all of the words from "*when*" to the word "*ringers*".

Grade 4 is the starting point characterizing narrators as being in the first, second, or third person. (The Grade 3 application of Reading Standard 6 is: "Distinguish their own point of view from that of the narrators.") This kind of terminology will be unfamiliar to fourth graders, although the concept itself is not that difficult to understand. I suggest using a chart that clearly illustrates examples of first person and third person narrative points of view, and have the students convert the language from one to the other to really learn this concept from the inside out.

Tip

As a rule, literature is not written in second person point of view. Occasionally, a character will step out momentarily and address the reader as "you," but this device is usually used within the first person point of view. For example, *The Adventures of Huckleberry Finn* opens with: "You don't know about me without you have read a book by the name of Tom Sawyer."

Such a chart might look like Figure 7.1, with sentences taken from three different points in the stories.

Now, as you'll see in Figure 7.2, it can be little more sophisticated to switch from third to first person because it becomes necessary to change the diction (word choice) and sentence structure so that it sounds like a real character speaking, rather than a detached narrator.

1st Person Point of View: *Hank the Cowdog, Book 1* by John R. Erickson

Original	Conversion to 3rd Person Point of View
It's me again. Hank the Cowdog. I just got some terrible news. There's been a murder on the ranch. (1)	Hank the Cowdog just got some terrible news. He just heard that there had been a murder on the ranch.
I sat up and opened my eyes. Bruno was getting a good scolding from his master. He whined and wagged his stump tail and tried to explain what had happened. But his master didn't understand. (This seems to be a common trait in masters.) (38).	Hank sat up and opened his eyes. Bruno was getting a good scolding from his master. Bruno whined and wagged his stump tail and tried to explain what had happened. But Bruno's master didn't understand. (This seems to be a common trait in masters.)
Well, as I've said before, every dog in this world isn't cut out for security work. It requires a keen mind, a thick skin, and a peculiar devotion to duty. I mean, you put in sixteen-eighteen hours a day. You're on call day and night. Your life is on the line every time you go out on patrol. You're doing jobs that nobody else wants to do because of the danger, etc. (127)	Every dog in this world isn't cut out for security work. It requires a thick skin, and a particular devotion to duty. Security work requires sixteen to eighteen hours a day. The security dog is on call day and night. His life is on the line every time he goes on patrol. He is doing jobs that nobody else wants to do because of the danger, etc.

Figure 7.1

3rd Person Point of View: *Julie of the Wolves* by Jean Craighead George

Original	Conversion to 1st Person Point of View
Miyax pushed back the hood of her sealskin parka and looked at the Arctic sun. It was a yellow disc in a lime-green sky, the colors of six o'clock in the evening and the time when the wolves awoke. Quietly she put down her cooking pot and crept to the top of the dome-shaped frost heave, one of the many earth buckles that rise and fall in the crackling cold of the Arctic winter. (3)	I pushed back the hood of my sealskin parka and looked at the Arctic sun. It was a yellow disc in a lime-green sky, so I knew that it was six o'clock in the evening. This was the time when the wolves awoke. Quietly, I put down my cooking put and crept to the top of one of many dome-shaped frost heaves. The Arctic winter is crackling cold, and many shapes like this one rise and fall in it.
The wind, the empty sky, the deserted earth—Miyax had felt the bleakness of being left behind once before (87).	With the wind blowing, the sky empty, and the earth deserted, again I felt how bleak it was to be left behind.

Figure 7.2

The plane swerved, dove, and skimmed about thirty feet above the ground. Its guns blasted. Amaroq stumbled, pressed back his ears, and galloped across the tundra like a shooting star. Then he reared, and dropped on the snow. He was dead. "For a bounty," she screamed. "For money, the magnificent Amaroq is dead!" Her throat constricted with grief, and sobs choked her.	I could see the plane swerve, dive, and skim about thirty feet above the ground. I could hear its guns blasting. Then, I saw Amaroq stumble, press back his ears, and gallop across the tundra. He was like a shooting star. Then he reared, and dropped on the snow. Amaroq was dead. I screamed. "For a bounty! For money!" They had killed the magnificent Amaroq and I could feel my throat close as my sobs choked me.

Figure 7.2 (Continued)

A few points to note about having students convert the point of view:

1. The students do not have to change the style from informal to formal. One of the key differences between narrative and informational text is the level of formality of the language. Even when expressed in the third person, narratives may be written in a conversational style. This means that slang, incorrect pronoun case, and incomplete sentences may be used in narrative text.

2. Don't hesitate to start small, with converting short, simple sentences into another narrative point of view.

3. Emphasize that most of the text will not change. The key changes will be in the pronouns alone. However, it is valuable to have the students copy the text directly because doing so reinforces their spelling, capitalization, punctuation, and sense of complete (and incomplete) sentences.

4. Sometimes, as in the *Hank the Cowdog* example, the pronoun *you* is employed to make general statements, not necessarily to address the reader. When this happens, convert the *you* statements into third person as demonstrated above.

5. As for quotation marks, you'll notice that I did not use them. This is because some of the text might use quotation marks within it to capture words of speakers, and I would run into the problem of then having to use single quotation marks. To avoid that confusion, I'm making the decision to dispense with quotation marks in this chart, which is permissible, because I've already indicated that I'm pulling words verbatim from a text. If this were part of a paragraph that I was writing, I couldn't dispense with the quotation marks, but, in this kind of a format, I can justify having students do that.

The rule: Use quotation marks when you pull text out to use within a paragraph that also contains your own words, so that the reader can distinguish your words from those of the text.

To explain this task to the students, your guiding questions are:

1. How would the story or information sound if it actually happened to you, but you were writing about it as if it happened to a character that you were making up? (3rd person)

2. How would the story or information sound if it actually happened to you, and you were writing about it? (1st person)

This activity connects to Writing Standard 3 to an extent, because it involves writing narratives, even though the students would not be writing original narratives, but playing with the language of a professional. If you look at some of the conversions above, you'll see that the opportunities for creative writing are definitely there as students re-fashion how a character might convey a thought through first person language.

Because students would need to use quotation marks (capitalization and commas) correctly when quoting the direct words of a character in context, we are also connecting to Language Standard 2, which addresses these conventions.

Applying Standard 6 to informational text at the fourth grade level can be done in the same way. Not all informational text is written in the third person. Students should be reading first person accounts of real events. They should also be noticing that directions are written in the second person, which is easy to recognize by the use of the pronoun *you* and by the use of sentences that are in the form of commands.

When students can identify whether a text is written in first or third person, when they can convert a text from one to the other, properly punctuated, then they are ready to move on to the Standards for Grades 5 and 6.

In Grade 5, students learn to "describe how a narrator's or speaker's point of view influences how events are described" (www.corestandards.org). What does this mean, as it relates to narrative text? Assuming that fifth grade students now are proficient at distinguishing between first and third person narrative point of view, consider the guiding questions for analysis:

1. If the narrative is written in the first person, how might the story be different if it were told through third person? In other words, if we are seeing the story only through the narrator's eyes, what might the narrator not be seeing? What might the narrator be interpreting in his or her own way? How might the truth be different from what the narrator (with the author pulling the strings) tells us directly? What might we know that the narrator

does not know? In real life, we can (sometimes) see the irony between a character's words and his or her actions. So, when a story is told through first person point of view, the reader is sometimes expected to see that same irony.

2. If the narrative is written in the third person, how might the story be different if told to us through any of the main or minor characters? Does the narrator seem to like or dislike particular characters? If the narrator presents a character in a negative light, surely that character would not see himself or herself that way! So, how would that character present himself or herself, if allowed to introduce *themselves* to the reader, rather than having the narrator skew the reader's opinion?

A perfect example is any novel written by Roald Dahl, an author who famously and hilariously portrays characters as evil and does so as a third person narrator. Here is the reader's introduction to Headmistress Agatha Trunchbull ("The Trunchbull") in *Matilda*:

> She was above all a most formidable female. She had once been a famous athlete, and even now the muscles were still clearly in evidence. You could see them in the bull-neck, in the big shoulders, in the thick arms, in the sinewy wrists and in the powerful legs. Looking at her, you got the feeling that this was someone who could bend iron bars and tear telephone directories in half. Her face, I'm afraid, was neither a thing of beauty nor a joy forever. She had an obstinate chin, a cruel mouth, and small arrogant eyes. (1988, p. 106)

A very negative first impression, indeed, but the author wants to make sure that we, as readers, understand that this character is a bully (hence her name). But if Headmistress Trunchbull were to introduce herself . . .? What words and images in the description might she replace, if she wanted to convey a more positive impression of herself? And, if her words about herself, conveyed in the first person, were to be at odds with what the reader knows as her actions, as well as how other characters describe her, then we would have the dramatic irony that often happens when a story is told in the first person. This kind of analysis connects to Language Standard 5 ("Demonstrate understanding of figurative language, word relationships, and nuances in word meanings") because it calls for an understanding of connotation not only of single words ("formidable," "obstinate," "cruel," "arrogant") but also of images ("bull-neck," "bend iron bars," "tear telephone directories in half.")

In Grade 5, reading Dahl's *Matilda*, a teacher addressing Reading Standard 6 would be working on ways to get the students to see that the author has given the reader a point of view that favors Matilda and Miss Honey, and that disfavors Matilda's parents and Headmistress Trunchbull.

In Grade 6, the students would be advancing from identifying point of view and understanding the effect of point of view upon the narrative. They would now "explain how the author develops the point of view of a speaker or narrator in text" (www.corestandards.org). The focus here is on the word *how*. An author uses various tools to develop the point of view through which the narrative is told. We want sixth graders to perceive two of these tools, which we've already addressed in grades 4 and 5:

Author's tools for developing a point of view in a narrative:

1. Narration: Is the story told in the first or third person? We can advance this concept in Grade 6 by refining the term *third person narrator*. Not all third person narrators have the same license to tell the story:

2.

- **A third person objective narrator** is like a real person to us, inasmuch as we can observe what other people around us do, we can hear what they say, but we cannot be certain of what is going on inside their heads. What that means is that we are on a ride-along as the story is being revealed. We cannot see into the mind of any of the characters, although we see everything through the perspective of the main character. This kind of narration is sometimes called the "dramatic narrator" or the "eye of the camera" because in a play, the audience doesn't usually interact directly with the characters. Rather, in a play, the characters go about their business, and the audience surmises their motivations and thoughts, as you would in real life. (In the works of Shakespeare, however, characters often speak directly to the audience, revealing their own thoughts in soliloquys or asides.) An accessible example of third person object point of view would be any of Aesop's fables. You are not being told what the tortoise or the hare is thinking, only what they would look like to the observer. You'll notice that stories told in this manner have lots of dialogue (because we can't see into the heads of the characters) and action verbs (because we have to see the action).

- **A third person limited narrator** has a brain's eye view inside the mind of the main character, but not the other characters. An example, from *Julie of the Wolves*: "A dull pain seized her stomach. She pulled blades of grass from their sheaths and ate the sweet ends. They were not very satisfying, so she picked a handful of caribou moss, a lichen. If the deer could survive in winter on this food, why not me? She munched, decided the plant might taste better if cooked, and went to the pond for water" (1972, p. 15). As you can see, this kind of narration is very similar to first person, in that we see inside of the mind of the main character. With this kind of narrative, expect to spend almost all of your time with the main character.

- **A third person omniscient narrator** gives us an all-access pass into the minds and through the walls of all of the characters and places. This is the most flexible and the most far-ranging point of view that an author can take. The third person omniscient narrator takes the reader into any nook or cranny where the story meanders. For example, *Charlotte's Web* (White, 1952) is written in the third person omniscient point of view. As readers, we get to see inside of the thoughts of Wilbur ("There's never anything to do around here, he thought.") as well as many of the other characters, including Charlotte ("Charlotte liked to do her weaving in the late afternoon. . . One afternoon she heard a most interesting conversation and witnessed a strange event" (p. 55).

Sixth graders would need copious examples of each of these third person points of view to begin to distinguish them. Some scaffolding questions:

1. Does the author tell you what characters are thinking? If the author does not tell you what any characters are thinking, but only what they are saying and doing, then the story is probably in the third person objective point of view.

2. If the author tells you what the characters are thinking, then the story is either in the third person limited point of view (only one character's thoughts are revealed) or the third person omniscient point of view (more than one character's thoughts are revealed).

3. Does the author take you to different places and time periods where the main character is not present? If so, then the story is probably in the third person omniscient point of view.

Here's how Standard 6 for literary text progresses into the 7–8 grade band:

To address Standard 6 at this level, you need to find literature that is complex enough to tell a story through different points of view (Grade 7) or has a narrator whose point of view differs from that of the author (Grade 8) with the intended result of either humor, suspense, or intensity of emotion that the reader feels as the story unfolds.

One of my favorite teachable stories for this grade level is O. Henry's "The Ransom of Red Chief." The humor of this story is all about the irony that is created through three points of view about the kidnapping of an obstreperous young boy: The kidnappers view the crime in its traditional sense, as a way of obtaining money through ransom. The young boy, Johnny, aka Red Chief, views it as an outdoor adventure and outlet for his usual demanding and annoying ways. And the father of the victim views the crime as an opportunity to demand a counter-ransom, offering to accept a fee from the kidnappers to take Johnny off their hands. The story is a perfect vehicle through which to teach irony.

For Grade 8, we're looking for an ironic difference between an author and the character he or she created. We want students to understand that just because a narrative is written in the first person, it is not to be assumed that the character's voice expresses the author's attitude. Especially with comical characters and villains, the character's voice can stand in ironic contrast to the author's hand. To see this difference, readers must develop awareness of the unreliable narrator—the narrator whose words are to be taken ironically.

We can use "The Ransom of Red Chief" as an example: It is narrated in the first person by one of the kidnappers. The intention of the narrator is to have us think of him as a savvy self-starter, an independent businessman who, along with his partner, decided that kidnapping the child of a prominent banker would be a profitable venture. He is altogether unconcerned with how the victims of his crime will be affected. Comically, the narrator assumes that we readers are on his side during the planning of the kidnapping and as it turns sour. The author wants us to think of the narrator differently: as a buffoon getting his just deserts for a dastardly act that goes awry, to our amusement.

One device that the author uses to convey irony is the misuse of multisyllabic words by the narrator and his partner. In the first paragraph, the narrator says: "It was, as Bill afterward expressed it, 'during a moment of temporary mental apparition'; but we didn't find that out till later" (p. 1). Eighth graders probably would not appreciate the ironic use of the word *apparition* in this context. To get them to see how an author creates irony in point of view, you would have to point out the deliberate misuse of this and other words in the story.

Informational Text

Now let's look at the progression for Reading Standard 6 for informational text in the 4–6 grade band:

Again, we always want to avoid referring to the author as "they." But when it comes to informational text, the definition of point of view is different than what it is for narrative text. We're not going to be talking about informational text in science or technical subjects for Standard 6. We can assume that straightforward, textbook-like information in these subjects is written objectively. When it comes to informational text and point of view, we'll be talking about the kind of authentic primary source documents that would be read for social studies. In these documents, the reader needs to know the perspective of the writer, and that perspective almost always has to do with social and personal circumstances and positions of power.

Accordingly, the essential questions for a primary source document, regarding Standard 6, begin with these (grades 4, 5):

Who wrote the document? What do we know about this person?
Who did the author expect would read this information? How do we know?
What was the author trying to accomplish by writing this document? How do we know?

In grades 4 and 5, we're teaching students how information and circumstances are viewed differently from people of different situations in life and different motivations for expressing themselves. Grade 6 becomes more analytical, with students learning how to examine how an author's language reveals his or her perspective and bias. Now would be the time to introduce the concept of connotation, the emotional effect of particular words. The best way to do this is through advertising. Have sixth graders examine the word choices in a written ad, identifying words having a positive or negative connotation.

In the 7–8 grade band levels, editorials are the perfect vehicle for these grade levels. There are three kinds of ideas that a reader of an editorial has to understand:

1. What is the subject of the editorial, and what is the background that a reader would need to know to understand it?

2. What is the editorialist's opinion and what are the reasons given for supporting this opinion?

3. What would be the opinion of those who disagree? Does the editorialist acknowledge (mention, recognize) opposing viewpoints?

Every debater and editorialist knows that part of mounting an effective argument is not to ignore opposing viewpoints, but to bring them up early in the argument, so as to neutralize them with a pre-emptive strike. This is done with signal words such as "although," and "even though" and with frames such as "Some may argue that. . ., but. . ." or "Granted that. . .; however. . ." We should direct students to these particular words and similar expressions to attune them to that part of Standard 6 that speaks of acknowledgement of opposing viewpoints.

As students analyze editorials by writing about them, they are working in Reading Standard 8 ("Delineate and evaluate the argument and specific claims in a text, including the validity of the reasoning as well as the relevance and sufficiency of the evidence.") and Writing Standard 8 ("Gather relevant information from multiple print and digital sources, assess the credibility and accuracy of each source, and integrate the information while avoiding plagiarism.").

As students move into the 9–10 grade band and beyond, they will be exploring specific rhetorical techniques (various types of figurative language and metaphors) in increasingly complex text.

Standard 6 Summary

Reading Standard 6 addresses point of view. In literary text, point of view refers broadly to whether the narrative is written in first person or third person. When reading a first person narrative, we may need to distinguish the narrator's perspective on events from that of the author, when the author creates a character with ironic intent. For informational text, point of view refers to the subjective stance that the author is taking toward the subject, and how the author uses connotative language and the other elements of argument to persuade the reader.

Guiding Questions for Readers: Standard 6

1. For literary text: How might the story be different if it were told from the point of view of a character other than the one chosen by the author to tell the story?

2. For informational text: Is the point of view objective or subjective? If subjective, what does the author want the readers to think positively and negatively about? Why? How do we know what the author's point of view is about the subject?

Reading Standards 7–9

Integration of Knowledge and Ideas

Reading Standards 7–9 are about using multiple texts to learn more about a single topic or version of a story. For these Standards, students are either comparing two or more texts, sometimes of different forms, or drawing knowledge about a given subject from two or more sources.

Reading Standard 7: Understand charts, graphs, and other numerical and visual information and media in addition to the words

Reading Standard 7: Integrate and evaluate content presented in diverse formats and media, including visually and quantitatively, as well as in words. (www.corestandards.org/ELA-Literacy/CCRA/R/7)

Tip

Keep some perspective: Where have students been, prior to Grade 4?

Grade 3: Literary: Explain how specific aspects of a text's illustrations contribute to what is conveyed by the words in a story (e.g., create mood, emphasize aspects of a character or setting).

Informational: Use information gained from illustrations (e.g., maps, photographs) and the words in a text to demonstrate understanding of the text (e.g., where, when, why, and how key events occur).

Where are students expected to go, after Grade 8?

Grades 9–10: Literary: Analyze the representation of a subject or a key scene in two different artistic media, including what is emphasized or absent in each treatment (e.g., Auden's "Musee des Beaux Arts" and Breughel's *Landscape with the Fall of Icarus*).

Informational: Analyze various accounts of a subject told in different media (e.g., a person's life story in both print and multimedia), determining which details are emphasized in each account.

Reading Standard 7 for Literary Text

The idea of Reading Standard 7 for literary text is for students to gain new dimensions of understanding by viewing, reading, or hearing different versions of a single story.

In Grade 4, students are expected to "make connections between the text of a story or drama and a visual or oral presentation of the text, identifying where each version reflects specific descriptions and directions in the text." Teachers lament that one of the problems with hewing to the Common Core's focus on text is the de-emphasis on viewing movies and theatrical presentations. Certainly, these are rich sources of cultural knowledge deserving their place in school. The good news is that we can continue to show quality movies and invite those wonderful traveling theatrical troupes to perform at assemblies. However, these experiences should not be wasted opportunities for sharpening critical thinking skills.

Teachers decide if the students are going to read the story before, after, or even interspersed with, viewing a performance. If they read it first, we can ask them to predict what specific parts of the story absolutely have to be included in the performance version of it, and which details may be left out. They can also find details in the text that create particular images—physical descriptions of characters and their clothing, details of the indoor and outdoor environment, and props that play a role in the advancing the plot. You'll notice that attending to these details in anticipation of a performance addresses the first two Reading Standards (close reading and distinguishing central themes from details). This kind of engagement is replicated in the eighth grade, on a more sophisticated level.

But performances rarely include everything in the written version. Minor characters disappear or are conflated with other characters, whole episodes are dispensed with, and casting decisions are surprising. These differences are opportunities to invite some evaluative thinking: Why did the screenplay writer or playwright leave this in and that out? And, was anything added that wasn't in the original? Why?

In fifth grade, students are evaluating production aesthetics: "Analyze how visual and multimedia elements contribute to the meaning, tone, or beauty of the text (e.g., graphic novel, multimedia presentation of fiction, folktale, myth, poem)." The thinking required here is very abstract because of the abstract nouns meaning, tone, and beauty. Let's talk about each of these:

- **Meaning:** To get a fifth grader to understand how "visual elements contribute to the meaning," we might show them a serious painting, a poster, movie trailer, or graphic novel panel and ask if seeing it helps them understand the words on the page. The sentence frame is: "This (picture) helps me understand the story better because it shows _____."

- **Tone:** We can make the concept of tone more accessible by starting with broad representations of tone, such as a dark and scary tone created by shading and images in a graphic novel: *How would you describe the feelings in these panels? How do you know?* and then: *"Look at the text. What words did the author use to convey such feelings?"* Only then should we introduce an abstract concept like *tone*: "What we've been talking about is called *tone*."

To teach the elusive concept of tone, you can even play the soundtrack of a movie version of a story that the class is reading and ask them to find the sentences in the text that correspond to the feelings evoked by the music.

And, again, because tone is such an abstract concept, students need to be given a vocabulary for it. Start with the most pronounced, easily identified tones: The tone is scary *(ominous, foreboding); cheerful (upbeat, optimistic, lively); sad (gloomy, glum); or peaceful (serene, carefree, tranquil).*

- **Beauty:** To a fifth grader, the word *beauty* means *prettiness.* To expand their understanding, we can explain that a story is said to be beautiful not only because it portrays visually pleasing people and things, but because the parts of it come together in the end like a jigsaw puzzle. The clicking together of rhyming lines, the humor of incongruity or exaggeration, the emotional response that we have when a story is well-craft, even the sense of lost time that we feel when a story absorbs us: These are expanded notions of beauty that can be clarified by nonprint versions of a text.

Reading Standard 7 in grades six, seven, and eight really give you a chance to show the films you like the students to see in your class and read the graphic novels. But you need to remember to anchor into the print versions either before or after, nurturing the academic vocabulary necessary to compare and contrast print to nonprint. Here is a sampling of such language:

Verbs: portray, depict, reveal, illustrate, expose, express, represent

Nouns: portrayal, depiction, expression, representation, close-up; scene, chapter, panel; mood, atmosphere

Adjectives: panoramic, detailed, expressive, suspenseful, dramatic

Remember that you can't just put these words up on a word wall or give brief definitions of them. Students can use these words to actually advance their thinking on Reading Standard 7, but only if you carefully, patiently, and persistently model how these words convey understanding of literature and nonprint media.

Reading Standard 7 for Informational Text

Reading Standard 7 for informational text is the one that connects most naturally to teachers of social studies, history, science, and technical subjects. Here is where we pay attention to the relationship between the words and the informational structures such as graphs, charts, diagrams, and maps that support the words.

Opportunities are everywhere in the local newspaper and throughout the curriculum. The first subject that comes to mind for learning to interpret data displays is math, of course. Having fourth graders go back and forth translating data displays into sentences, and vice versa, is the natural connection between math and Reading Standard 7 (and Writing Standard 2, writing explanatory texts).

But math is not the only place for Reading Standard 7: Science and social studies deal with classification systems that can be displayed in matrices. Science and social studies textbooks are organized in ways that translate easily into outlines. Translating a textbook chapter into an outline is the perfect way to process, remember, and study it.

Fourth graders (and up) can integrate Reading Standard 7 both as a means for learning and a format for expressing knowledge (assessment):

1. Timelines
2. Flow charts
3. Maps
4. Bar graphs, pie charts, scattergrams
5. Scores and surveys
6. Cycles
7. Diagrams of structures
8. Matrices of classifications
9. Quadrants
10. Reference tables
11. Recipe charts, showing different portions
12. Running records
13. Rubrics
14. Product labels

In keeping with my maxim that verbs are the engine of language (and thinking), here is a starter kit of verbs for interpreting data:

represent
express
display
increase, decrease
develop

I'll say again, learning to use these verbs happens through modeling and practice. These verbs should be treated as utensils, not wallpaper (my term for underused word walls), not vocabulary words to be quizzed on and soon dismissed, not novelties. As with all utensils, the inexperienced user is awkward at first, unable to manipulate or improvise. If fourth graders took the entire school year to become fully competent on these six verbs to interpret data, that would be an accomplishment that would lay the groundwork for all kinds of analytical thinking that will serve them well throughout their lives.

Fifth graders are expected to use non-verbal data to solve problems quickly. This involves experience in the genres and the ability to immediately orient themselves to various kinds of organizational structures. However, fifth graders need to learn not to jump into the illustration without first understanding the purpose of the data and the organizational structure (keys, legends, headings, color codes, etc.). Essential questions to be asked *before* any answers are found are:

What does this (graph, chart, table, map, etc.) represent?

How is it organized? (The columns represent_____, and rows represent_____; The main heading is_____, and the subheadings are_____.

Sixth graders are being asked to integrate numerical or diagrammatic information with verbal text to build knowledge on a topic. This implies the creation of a written report or presentation on a simple topic that involves numbers and/or some kind of diagram (or map). Having a diagram or statistics to refer to not only enhances the content and credibility of an oral presentation, but it also reduces the anxiety of having to face an audience without any props.

For some reason, Reading Standard 7 for informational text moves away from numbers, asking students to compare and contrast verbal information from different forms. The example given is the difference between the text of a speech and the actual performance of it. This is the perfect opportunity for ELA and social studies teachers to collaborate, using the great American speeches that we have on video or film.

This leads to the evaluative component of Grade 8, in which students are asked to consider the advantages and disadvantages of different media. Clips of science-related movies and documentaries can be compared to corresponding textbook information: *What new understandings do we get from seeing the film? What information is in the text that is not depicted in the film?*

Standard 7 Summary

Reading Standard 7 is about experiencing a story or building knowledge through text *and* at least one other medium, enhancement, or format. This is the Standard that, while it may be least familiar to traditional English teachers, is most familiar to teachers of other subjects, especially math. This is also the Standard that allows English teachers to use video and film in a way that connects to, and does not replace, text, as we make students stronger readers.

Guiding Questions for Readers: Standard 7

1. For literary text: What parts of the text are not included or added in the film version? Why do you suppose these changes were made?

2. For informational text: How does the graphic information (chart, graph, table, map, etc.) help you understand the words in the text?

Reading Standard 8: Judge the Validity of Arguments

Reading Standard 8: Delineate and evaluate the argument and specific claims in a text, including the validity of the reasoning as well as the relevance and sufficiency of the evidence. (www.corestandards.org/ELA-Literacy/CCRA/R/8)

Reading Standard 8 is applicable only to informational text, not literary text.

Tip

Keep some perspective: Where have students been, prior to Grade 4?

Grade 3: Describe the logical connection between particular sentences and paragraphs in a text (e.g., comparison, cause/effect, first/second/third in a sequence).

Where are students expected to go, after Grade 8?

Grades 9–10: Delineate and evaluate the argument and specific claims in a text, assessing whether the reasoning is valid and the evidence is relevant and sufficient; identify false statements and fallacious reasoning.

Reading Standard 8 and Writing Standard 1

Reading Standard 8 (judging the validity of arguments based on their claims and the support for the claims) is the reciprocal skill to Writing Standard 1 ("Write arguments to support claims . . ."). A student's ability to write a sturdy argument will be shaped by the models of argumentation that the student has read, analyzed, and evaluated. As students move up the grade levels, reading increasingly complex arguments, they should be accumulating the necessary rhetorical vocabulary, as suggested in the following grade-by-grade progression.

But before we get to that, let's consider some age-appropriate readings for argumentation. Argumentation is one genre that definitely requires significant background knowledge, especially about current events. Beginning in Grade 4 (if not before), students should have access to age-appropriate, well-written opinion pieces, such as can be found in any of the Scholastic Magazines for science and social studies.

According to the Reading Standards, students coming in to Grade 4 should have a basic vocabulary to describe intra-textual connections: recognition of comparison/contrast, sequential, and cause and effect structures. From there, we should probably focus on cause and effect—cause and effect relationships can be easily recognizable (and producible) through the word *because*.

The evidence for the claim that _____ is _____ is that_____.

If you are thinking: "A fourth grade would never come up with a sentence like this," you'd be right, and that is the point of providing the sentence frame. The sentence frame scaffolds thinking. With a sentence frame like this, the fourth grader, with help, can think analytically about claims and evidence. (Without it, the fourth grader will probably get tangled up in words or will default to telling what the text is about, rather than analyzing it for claim(s) and evidence.)

Let's ease into analyzing claims and evidence with something that fourth graders can access. The "Goofus and Gallant" cartoons have been around in *Highlights for Children Magazine* since 1948. (In case you don't know the form: There are two cartoon boxes, each representing the results of either gentlemanly (Gallant), or boorish (Goofus) behavior in the same situation.) The claim is that a given kind of considerate behavior has happy results for all concerned; selfish, unmannerly behavior in the same situation has the opposite result. The evidence is clearly depicted by two different illustrations, respectively.

Tip

Understanding what the word *claim* means: To analyze arguments, students need a working understanding of the word *claim*, the word used repeatedly in Reading Standard 8 and Writing Standard 1. This word is tricky because it is used to express various meanings: to *claim* something from the lost and found; to *claim* the ability to do something; to *claim* the truth or existence of something. There are economic uses of claim that children might have heard their parents use: to file an insurance *claim,* to *claim* dependents on a tax document, to have a legal *claim*. Dictionary definitions won't clarify the meaning of the word in the Reading Standard 8/Writing Standard 1 context. Let's use age-appropriate working definitions of *claim*, definitions which we can refine as students develop proficiency in understanding abstract concepts. For now, let's just define *claim* as "something that must be proven with evidence." So, if you claim to love lamb chops, you have to eat them, but that is not the kind of claim we are interested in. We are interested in the kinds of claims that have to be proven with hard facts outside of your own preferences.

Fourth graders can read articles that present arguments about everyday subjects such as fire safety, bullying, nutrition and fitness, and environmental concerns. To address Reading Standard 8, they should learn how to use the

(This sentence frame may surprise you because it uses *is* twice. However, I do recommend the use of non-action verbs for circumstances just such as this: This is not an action sentence. This is a sentence that stays put, simply making a stable declaration of fact.)

words *claim, reason,* and *evidence.* They should learn how to use the word *claim* as both a noun and a verb.

In fifth grade, Reading Standard 8 hones in to having students match reasons and evidence to claims, which is not much of a leap from what they've done in fourth grade.

Beginning in sixth grade, students need to discern claims that are supported by reasons and evidence from those that are not. This is similar to distinguishing facts from opinions and reason from emotion. The language of the grade-level standard, specifically the use of the word *trace,* indicates that the arguments that sixth graders are expected to read are longer than those read up to this point. An argument that is long enough to be "traced" probably consists of anecdotes, examples, cause and effect statements, and other rhetorical elements comprising its "ingredients."

For seventh graders, we need to start teaching about the elements of logical thinking so that students may ". . . assess whether the reasoning is sound and the evidence relevant and sufficient to support the claims." To do this kind of assessment, students need to learn a primer of concepts (and the terms that name them) about logic and critical thinking. Up to now, students have been evaluating information by making broad statements like, "This doesn't make sense," and "This guy doesn't know what he's talking about," "I don't like this," and the all-purpose, "This is stupid." If statements like these are the go-to vocabulary for Reading Standard 8, anything we teach them about the language of logic will be a significant step in the right direction. Let's begin with these:

1. Is the author dodging the issues and diverting your attention by making a personal attack? This is called an *ad hominem* attack (literally, Latin for "to the man"). Critical thinkers recognize *ad hominem* attacks as unfair play. Rather than strengthening an argument, they detract from it and reduce the credibility of the person making them.

2. Is the author setting up a false link of cause to effect? Just because the rooster crows at dawn does not mean that the rooster *causes* the dawn. Correlation is not causation.

3. Is the author using incendiary (highly emotional) language that seems designed to rev up your emotions (fear, anger, pity, guilt) to divert you from the facts?

4. Is the argument based on a sound premise? A premise is the underlying assumption upon which the argument rests. Some teachers refer to premises as warrants. A premise (or a warrant) is something that makes sense and is generally agreed upon, such as: *People deserve equal rights. Companies should sell products that are safe and reliable. Parents and schools should set good examples for children.*

These four concepts, abstract as they are, will not be easy to teach to seventh or eighth graders. Fortunately, the eighth grade expectations are barely distinguishable from those of the seventh grade, leaving us a full two years to get students to become conversant on these basic elements of logic and critical thinking.

There is an inherent contradiction in Reading Standard 8: In asking students to recognize specious elements of arguments that they read, we're assuming that they *are* reading arguments that are less than credible. But students need copious models of good—not faulty—argumentation. It is difficult for anyone to be objective and analytical about the issues we usually read about. In authentic reading situations, we usually choose to read arguments (editorials, for examples) about issues that we care about. Our biases get in the way of our objectivity. Also, we have background knowledge that students lack. So, the question is: Where can we obtain written arguments that give students the authentic opportunities to find arguments that do not stand up to criteria for validity? (Without such reading, we really are not doing justice to Reading Standard 8.) Try letters to the editor about local and familiar issues. These are usually short and often written in language that relies on emotional and personal response rather than the elements of reasoning that students are learning.

Standard 8 Summary

Reading Standard 8 requires a unique perspective. While the other Reading Standards for informational text require the processing of information at face value, Reading Standard 8 requires that the reader question the objective truth of the text.

Guiding Questions for Readers: Standard 8

1. As far as the reader knows, is the information accurate?

2. Is the author using a language register and diction that contribute to credibility?

3. Is the author fair to opposing arguments?

4. Is the author manipulative or insulting the intelligence of the reader?

5. Is there sufficient depth and support in the argument?

6. Does the author demonstrate a true grasp of the subtleties and facts of the issue?

7. Does the author give rightful credit to respectable sources to bolster the argument?

8. Is the author serious and rational, rather than glib and extreme?

9. Is the information in the text coherent or are parts of it irrelevant, disconnected, unexplained, or contradictory?

Reading Standard 9: Text Comparisons

Reading Standard 9: Analyze how two or more texts address similar themes or topic in order to build knowledge or to compare the approaches the authors take. (www.corestandards.org/ELA-Literacy/CCRA/R/9)

For Reading Standard 9, there is significant difference between literary and informational text. For literary text, students must dig into genre features, themes, literary elements, and author's style as well as the content of the texts being compared. That is what is meant by the words ". . . compare the approaches the authors take." For informational text, students need to attend only to the information given in two or more texts. This is what is meant by the words ". . . to build knowledge." In this chapter, we'll be looking at how to teach students how to compare literary texts analytically; how to extract information from two informational texts on the same subject, synthesizing relevant information into a report; *and* how to analyze a hybrid of literary and informational text about the same subject.

Tip

Keep some perspective: Where have students been, prior to Grade 4?

Grade 3: Literary: Compare and contrast the themes, settings, and plots of stories written by the same author about the same or similar characters (e.g., in books from a series). (www.corestandards.org/ELA-Literacy/RL/3)

Informational: Compare and contrast the most important points and key details presented in two texts on the same topic. (www.corestandards.org/ELA-Literacy/RI/3)

Teaching Reading Standard 9 for Literary Text

Comparing Themes

Reading Standard for Grade 3 gives the example of the theme of good vs. evil. Certainly, that is a prevalent theme in the literature that children have experienced so far in their education and exposure to stories. We can start by looking at how authors shape our understanding about villains, since villains not only drive the story, but are endlessly fascinating:

1. **First impressions:** Authors portray villains by creating scary first impressions. Fourth graders can set up vocabulary charts that compare the words that the authors use to introduce us to the villains, including their physical characteristics, where they live, who surrounds and serves them, and their actions and motivations.

2. **Victories:** The endings of stories whose theme is good vs. evil often end in similar ways. Do our heroes/heroines live happily ever after by vanquishing the villain?

3. **Helpers:** Often in children's stories, the protagonist has an ally. Whether it is a fairy godmother, wizard, some other guiding force, fourth graders can look at the role of this ally. The major role of most story-book allies, although they intervene in times of emergency, like parents, is to fortify the protagonist with his or her own untried powers.

4. **Differences:** Is one villain human and the other non-human? Is one villain physically attractive and the other is monstrous? Does one villain have a soft spot—even a lovable quality—while the other is evil through and through? Does one villain operate primarily by the brain and the other by brawn? Does one villain preside over minions while the other is a lone wolf?

Other common themes in children's and young adult literature are overcoming fears, not necessarily of evil opponents, but perhaps of unfamiliar ones—a new school or family structure, for example; the challenges of friendship and peer pressure; coping with illness or disability.

Literary themes, as we've discussed (Reading Standard 2), often coincide with predictable structures: the coming-of-age story, the road trip and fish-out-of-water structure. Students can map similarities in themes and structures using the familiar Freytag model, in which a line graph represents key turning points in a story: exposition (what happens before the curtain actually comes up on the story), inciting incident (aka, Plot Point 1, the point at which the equilibrium of the main character's world is broken and things start to get interesting, propelling the character towards a strong but thwarted desire), rising action (a series of incidents in which the main character undergoes setbacks and has to marshal heretofore undiscovered strengths to achieve the goal), climax (the point at which the main character is at the point of no return and something must change, soon and drastically), reversal (moment of insight, and carrying out the surprising result of that insight), falling action (tidying up), and conclusion (resolution, in which the main character returns to the physical starting point, not fitting in anymore because of newfound wisdom). Any point on this model can be the focus of comparison between two stories.

Comparing Themes *and* Topics

Beginning in Grade 4 and into Grade 5, students are expected to compare not only themes but also topics between two works of literature. In Grade 5, the Reading Standard is specific about focusing on subgenres of literature such as mysteries, adventure stories, horror stories, sports stories, stories about preteens and teenagers, or series books by the same author. The trick is to differentiate between topic and theme (Reading Standard 2) and to begin to see how the topic *carries* the theme(s).

Using mystery stories as an example, the *topic* might be a particular type of crime (murder, theft, kidnapping, etc.); a *theme* might be "life in the Big City" or "children notice more than adults" or "key clues come from where you'd least expect to find them" or "there's no such thing as coincidence." As we've said, a theme is only a theme if it is a repeated, cohesive, and therefore unifying element of the story. And the *approach* could be the point of view from which the story is told (Reading Standard 6), whether the reader knows the inside story of the crime and is watching the detectives and/or victims solve it themselves or whether it is structured as a who-done-it, with the reader as the detective, perceiving or ignoring inferences (clues).

Using adventure stories as an example, the *topic* might be prospecting for gold in Alaska, mountain-climbing in Tibet, or camping in the wilds; a *theme* might be the MacGiver-like invention of life-saving devices, wanting to give up, discovering the wonders of nature, or the physical weakness but mental acuity of the human compared to animals. And the *approach* could be the point of view from which the adventure is told (Reading Standard 6), how the timeline is rolled out (present or past tense? flashbacks or straight chronology?), or how the adventure came about (a planned and purposeful expedition? Or did it happen to the characters as a result of an accident, mistake, or misunderstanding?).

Comparing Themes and Topics in Different Genres

Beginning in Grade 6, students learn how to compare literary forms (genres) that address similar themes and topics. Students can compare the topics and themes of Langston Hughes' poem "A Dream Deferred" to the Lorraine Hansbury play *A Raisin in the Sun* whose title is lifted from that poem. This would be a *thematic* comparison. A *topical* comparison would be to compare Gary Paulsen's novel

Woodsong, a true story about the author's experience running the Iditerod, to John Greenleaf Whittier's poem "Snowbound."

Many literature anthologies organize selections thematically, while others organize by genre. Thematic arrangements are convenient for Reading Standard 9. In textbook anthologies, you'll find broad themes. For example, the Glencoe Literature series (Glencoe McGraw-Hill), Course 3 organizes its literature around eight themes: the concept of home, the ups and downs of friendship, finding direction in life, trickery, the pursuit of freedom, insightful moments, people worth admiring, and horror stories.

Thematic organization makes it easy to compare works of different genres on the same theme . . . *too* easy. We need to help students perceive common themes in literature of different genres without telling them from the outset what the themes are (as anthologies do). To scaffold to this level, we start by having them read thematically-related literature where they know the themes in advance. We can then mix the literature in the anthology, asking them to find, let's say, the theme of "the meaning of home" in a work of literature that is not in that unit, but that expresses that theme anyway. ("Put on your theme glasses and find . . ."). For example, in the Glencoe anthology, "The Diary of Anne Frank" (Goodrich and Hackett, 1959), which is Anne Frank's diary treated as a dramatic script, appears in the thematic unit about people worth admiring ("Faces of Dignity"). But certainly, the "meaning of home" theme pervades it as well. Similarly, an excerpt from James Herriott's autobiographical *All Things Bright and Beautiful* appears in the unit about the ups and downs of friendship ("Lean on Me"), but it certainly connects to the themes of moments of insight, and even trickery. Finally, we want students to, without scaffolding, perceive themes between two (or more) works of literature on the same theme without being told what the themes are, which builds upon Reading Standard 2.

Vocabulary of Literary Genres

The language of literary genres is a bit complicated, and some of the terms are overlapping. In its broadest sense, the word *genre* means *kind of,* and is used specifically for art forms (literature, music and the performing arts, the visual arts). In literature, the two broadest categories are *fiction* and *nonfiction*, but some writers, such as Truman Capote in *In Cold Blood*, blur the lines between them by adding fictitious elements to a true story, creating a hybrid form. We can also choose to divide literature into the two broad categories of prose and poetry. As with fiction and nonfiction, there's plenty of crossover: Prose may drip with poetic elements and exude a poetic feel; poetry doesn't necessarily rhyme or have a sing-song rhythm. But, as with fiction and nonfiction, whether literature is to be considered prose or poetry depends more on the way the author wants us to receive it than upon clear-cut features. Drama, another genre, may be written as poetry (*Romeo and Juliet*) and may tell a true story (*The Diary of Anne Frank*) and may be nonfiction at its spine but embellished with fictitious episodes (*Saint Joan*).

We can also divide literature into the two broad genres of comedy and tragedy. In the narrowest sense, a comedy is not just a story that makes us laugh, nor is a tragedy a story with a sad ending. A comedy is a tale, funny or not, that ends on an upbeat note. (A reader looking for laughs in Dante's *The Divine Comedy* would be disappointed . . . probably.) A tragedy tells the story of the downfall of a powerful and honorable person, a person on whom a social unit depends, because of a personal but very human failing known as a tragic flaw.

On a more granular level, we have subgenres. Fictional stories may be mysteries, adventures, fantasy, romances, et al., in terms of content. They may be categorized as children's stories, or young adult literature (YAL), or by form: graphic novels. Fiction may be categorized by length: novels, novellas, short stories, short short stories. We have historical novels, defined by the creation of fictitious characters who play against a background inspired by true settings and events.

And on an even more granular level, we have subcategories of the subgenres: the gothic novel, the bildungsroman (coming-of-age story about the psychological, intellectual, or spiritual maturation of the main character), even something called the roman a clef (a novel about real people and places masked with fictitious names).

However, just because genres may blend, we should teach students to be accurate when speaking about literature. Most of all, we should teach them not to name every kind of book as a novel: Collections of essays, biographies and autobiographies, and memoirs should never be referred to as *novels*.

But the spirit of Reading Standard 9 is probably to compare broad categories of genres—prose, poetry, drama—to each other, where the themes and/or topics are the same. What about having students compare a novel to the movie version of it? I would say that doing so is a justifiable way to address Reading Standard 9 if class time is not used to show an entire full-length movie. I say this because 120 minutes of class time lost to the viewing of a movie is not a Standards-based use of time. Furthermore, breaking up a movie into several pieces shown over several days is not the intended use of the medium. However, we can select relevant *segments* of a film and compare them to the corresponding *segment* of novel upon which it is based. We can also have students compare books read as part of the curriculum (a combination of in-class and for-homework reading) to a movie that they watch *at home*.

Comparing Portrayals of History: Fiction vs. Nonfiction

Beginning in Grade 7, students compare a fictional portrayal of an event (place, or character) in history to a nonfiction account of it. This evokes Reading Standard 6 (the significance of point of view). Specifically, students must express their understanding of "how authors use or alter history" in their creation of literature. This is the perfect place for coordination between the social studies and English language arts curriculum.

A unit in the social studies textbook addresses a period of history, presenting information in chronological order, detailing the key individuals and groups that defined the period, including authentic visuals and primary source documents. The best social studies textbooks have been thoughtfully constructed to represent various perspectives—from those in power to ordinary folks who were affected, positively and negatively, by the decisions of those in power. There are depictions, in the form of anecdotes, illustrations, and illustrations of works of art, of both everyday life and world-changing events. Reading Standard 9 serves to extend and deepen what students learn from the social studies textbook by adding the dimension of literature.

It is at this point that students should learn how to use words like *portray/ portrayal, from the perspective of,* and *through the eyes of* to compare a fictionalized re-creation of a historical event with an account of it that purports to be nonfiction.

A historical novel is a work of fiction (novel) whose author did not live in the time and place in which the novel took place. (*Great Expectations* and *Oliver Twist* are not historical novels. Charles Dickens wrote them about the time and place in which he actually lived. *A Tale of Two Cities,* however, is a historical novel, as Dickens himself was not living during the French Revolution.) For generations, *Johnny Tremain,* Esther Forbes' historical novel about how a young Boston teenager was affected by the American Revolution, has been a pillar of the seventh grade curriculum. It works perfectly for Reading Standard 9.

Comparing Versions of a Single Story

Beginning in Grade 8, students learn to compare versions of a single story. Folktales, fables, fairy tales, and myths work well for this application of Reading Standard 9. But presenting students with two versions of the same story is not enough: We need to teach eighth graders the vocabulary that is necessary to discuss an author's style.

In comparing two versions of a single story, the points of comparison begin with the literary elements: character, setting, conflict and plot, theme, narrative point of view: Are there details, such as minor characters or events, presented in one version and not the other? Are the quoted words of the characters the same in both versions? Are the endings exactly the same? Often, when an author adapts an ancient story, such as a folktale, fairy tale, fable, or myth, he or she will make substitutions so that the story will fit in to its intended culture: Consider the different versions of Cinderella.

This might be the perfect place to fit graphic novels into the curriculum. Graphic versions of very challenging literature, such as Shakespearean plays, can be very helpful in getting students to understand, and therefore become drawn into, great stories whose language is more complex than students could handle without the visuals in the graphic versions.

Graphic organizer charts that show the key literary elements and how they are portrayed in the two versions of the same story can be helpful for this task.

Reading Standard 9 and Informational Text

When it comes to informational text, Reading Standard 9 is governed by two connected questions throughout the grade levels: *What do I want to know? How do I go about finding it in these two (or more) texts?* Reading Standard 9 is directly linked to Writing Standard 8, "Gather relevant information from multiple print and digital sources, and integrate the information while avoiding plagiarism" (www.commoncore.org).

The comparison, then, is not for its own sake, as it is when comparing literary text, but for the practical purpose of accessing needed information from two sources. To teach for that, we need to make students aware of the structure of informational texts: where key information and supportive details are usually found within it. Encyclopedia-type reference materials, whole books on a single topic, and picture books are good sources for meeting Reading Standard 9.

Tip

Perspective: Where are students expected to go, after Grade 8?

Grades 9–10: Literary: Analyze how an author draws from and transforms material in a specific work (e.g., how Shakespeare treats a theme or topic from Ovid or the Bible or how a later author draws on a play by Shakespeare).

Informational: Analyze seminal U.S. documents of historical and literary significance (e.g., Washington's Farewell Address, the Gettysburg Address, Roosevelt's Four Freedoms speech, King's "Letter from the Birmingham Jail"), including how they address related themes and concepts.

Standard 9 Summary

Reading Standard 9 involves having students compare and contrast two or more texts that address the same topic and/or themes. For literary text, there are specific grade-by-grade requirements as to how this standard is to be applied. And, for literary text, students need to learn how to analyze text in terms of both content and style. (Style may be defined as the author's word choice, especially whether the word choice is formal or informal.) For informational text, the expectations from grade to grade remain the same—that students learn to extract information about a single topic from at least two texts—while the level of complexity increases.

Guiding Questions for Readers: Standard 9

1. For literary text: How does the content of two stories (dramas, poems) compare in terms of content (subject matter)? How do they compare in terms of form (genre, organization, language style)?

2. For informational text: What information do we learn about a given topic from each of the sources that we read about it?

Reading Standard 10

Range of Reading and Level of Text Complexity

Reading Standard 10: Reading and comprehending complex literary and informational text independently and proficiently.

Reading Standard 10 is the culmination of the other Anchor Standards. You'll note that the key descriptors are the adverbs *independently* and *proficiently*, and, of course, the adjective *complex*. By *independently*, we mean without scaffolding; by *proficiently*, we mean having the ability to gather information and answer questions addressed by the other nine Reading Standards. And students need to become independent and proficient with text that meets the grade band complexity targets (as delineated by the Common Core document (www. corestandards.org/ELA-Literacy/CCRA/R/10).

As I see it, four educational experiences are the most important in bringing students to Reading Standard 10:

1. **Informational and verbal proficiency:** Because background knowledge and vocabulary are critical to comprehension of any kind, the school-wide educational program needs to expose students to rich academic vocabulary in the context of learning the subject areas. While it is true that learners need to connect new information to that which is familiar, we all need to be conscious of the need to constantly and persistently introduce students to new words, new sights, new concepts, new stories, new facts, new uses of language, new figures of speech.

    As the saying goes, every time students leave a classroom having learned something about this great big world, they have become better readers. Strategies cannot compensate for a paucity of background knowledge and vocabulary.

2. **Guided practice with complex text:** There is definitely a place for whole class and small group study of complex text, where students are doing more than just answering text-dependent questions. Text-dependent questions need to be grounded in Reading Standards 1–6 for single passages; and Reading Standards 7–9 for multiple readings that are being brought together under one theme or topic.

3. **Free reading:** Just as strategies are useless without background knowledge and vocabulary, guided reading of complex text will not bring students to the necessary level of skill without substantial independent reading to pursue interests. Just because the Reading Standards focus on meticulous reading of academic texts, that doesn't mean that students, like us, also need to read casually. Skimming, scanning, and sampling are other forms of reading that are valuable by themselves, and that build vocabulary, fluency, background knowledge, and models of well-written sentences. English class should not be the only class associated with casual reading. Particularly in science and the humanities, students should be offered interesting, accessible articles, book excerpts, and even whole books.

4. **Teaching reading and writing as skills that are mutually supporting:** According to the University of Chicago Consortium on Chicago School Research, the most important educational practice in the K–12 curriculum to prepare students for college is writing across the disciplines (aka content area writing). The findings suggest that students need to write across the disciplines at least five times per month. Writing that defends a point of view with evidence is especially beneficial.

Standard 10 Summary

The Reading Standards pull in the other Literacy Standards, which are for Writing, Listening and Speaking, and Language (Grammar and Vocabulary). Because reading is a skill, it can be strengthened by practice. The practice needs to come from several directions:

1. Guided whole class demonstrations of how to tackle complex text;

2. Small group problem-solving sessions, where the problem to be solved depends on close reading of text and applying background knowledge;

3. Open reading sessions in all subject areas in which students are free to pursue their interests through casual reading (skimming, scanning, sampling).

Guiding Questions for Readers: Standard 10

1. Can I explain what I've read to someone else?

2. What challenges did I face in reading this? What did I do as a reader to address these challenges?

3. Am I getting better as a reader? How do I know?

Appendix A

The Reading Standards, Grade by Grade

(www.corestandards.org)

Grade 4

Reading Standard 1:

For literary and informational text: Refer to details and examples in a text when explaining what the text says explicitly and when drawing inferences from the text.

Reading Standard 2:

For literary text: Determine the theme of a story, drama, or poem from details in the text; summarize the text.

For informational text: Determine the main idea of a text and explain how it is supported by key details; summarize the text.

Reading Standard 3:

For literary text: Describe in depth a character, setting, or event in a story or drama, drawing on specific details in the text (e.g., a character's thoughts, words, or actions).

For informational text: Explain events, procedures, ideas, or concepts in a historical, scientific, or technical text, including what happened and why, based on specific information in the text.

Reading Standard 4:

For literary text: Determine the meaning of words and phrases as they are used in a text, including those that allude to significant characters found in mythology (e.g., Herculean).

For informational text: Determine the meaning of general academic and domain-specific words or phrases in a text relevant to a Grade 4 topic or subject area.

Reading Standard 5:

For literary text: Explain major differences between poems, drama, and prose, and refer to the structural elements of poems (e.g., verse, rhythm, meter) and drama (e.g., casts of characters, settings, descriptions, dialogue, stage directions) when writing or speaking about a text.

For informational text: Describe the overall structure (e.g., chronology, comparison, cause/effect, problem/solution) of events, ideas, concepts, or information in a text or part of a text.

Reading Standard 6:

For literary text: Compare and contrast the point of view from which different stories are narrated, including the difference between first- and third-person narrations.

For informational text: Compare and contrast a firsthand and second-hand account of the same event or topic; describe the differences in focus and the information provided.

Reading Standard 7:

For literary text: Make connections between the text of a story or drama and a visual or oral presentation of the text, identifying where each version reflects specific descriptions in the text.

For informational text: Interpret information presented visually, orally, or quantitatively (e.g., in charts, graphs, diagrams, time lines, animations, or interactive elements in Web pages) and explain how the information contributes to an understanding of the text in which it appears.

Reading Standard 8:

For literary text: (does not apply)

For informational text: Explain how an author uses reasons and evidence to support particular points in a text.

Reading Standard 9:

For literary text: Compare and contrast the treatment of similar themes and topics (e.g., opposition of good and evil) and patterns of events (e.g., the quest) in stories, myths, and traditional literature from different cultures.

For informational text: Integrate information from two texts on the same topic in order to write or speak about the subject knowledgeably.

Reading Standard 10:

For literary text: By the end of the year, read and comprehend literature, including stories, dramas, and poetry, in the grades 4–5 complexity band proficiently, with scaffolding as needed at the high end of the range.

For informational text: By the end of the year, read and comprehend informational texts, including history/social studies, science, and technical texts, in the grades 4–5 text complexity band proficiently, with scaffolding as needed at the high end of the range.

Grade 5

Reading Standard 1:

For literary and informational text: Quote accurately from a text when explaining what the text says explicitly and when drawing inferences from the text.

Reading Standard 2:

For literary text: Determine a theme of a story, drama, or poem from details in the text, including how characters in a story or drama respond to challenges or how the speaker in a poem reflects upon a topic; summarize the text.

For informational text: Determine two or more main ideas of a text and explain how they are supported by key details; summarize the text.

Reading Standard 3:

For literary text: Compare and contrast two or more characters, settings, or events in a story or drama, drawing on specific details in the text (e.g., how characters interact).

For informational text: Explain the relationships or interactions between two or more individuals, events, ideas, or concepts in a historical, scientific, or technical text based on specific information in the text.

Reading Standard 4:

For literary text: Determine the meaning of words and phrases as they are used in a text, including figurative language such as metaphors and similes.

For informational text: Determine the meaning of general academic and domain-specific words and phrases in a text relevant to a Grade 5 topic or subject area.

Reading Standard 5:

For literary text: Explain how a series of chapters, scenes, or stanzas fits together to provide the overall structure of a particular story, drama, or poem.

For informational text: Compare and contrast the overall structure (e.g., chronology, comparison, cause/effect, problem/solution) of events, ideas concepts, or information in two or more texts.

Reading Standard 6:

> **For literary text:** Describe how a narrator's or speaker's point of view influences how events are described.

> **For informational text:** Analyze multiple accounts of the same event or topic, noting important similarities and differences in the point of view they represent.

Reading Standard 7:

> **For literary text:** Analyze how visual and multimedia elements contribute to the meaning, tone, or beauty of a text (e.g., graphic novel, multimedia presentation of fiction, folktale, myth, poem).

> **For informational text:** Draw on information from multiple print or digital sources, demonstrating the ability to locate an answer to a question quickly or to solve a problem efficiently.

Reading Standard 8:

> **For literary text:** (does not apply)

> **For informational text:** Explain how an author uses reasons and evidence to support particular points in a text, identifying which reasons and evidence support which point(s).

Reading Standard 9:

> **For literary text:** Compare and contrast stories in the same genre (e.g., mysteries and adventure stories) on their approaches to similar themes and topics.

> **For informational text:** Integrate information from several texts on the same topic in order to write or speak about the subject knowledgeably.

Reading Standard 10:

> **For literary text:** By the end of the year, read and comprehend literature, including stories, dramas, and poetry, in the grades 4–5 complexity band proficiently.

> **For informational text:** By the end of the year, read and comprehend informational texts, including history/social studies, science, and technical texts, in the grades 4–5 text complexity band proficiently.

Grade 6

Reading Standard 1:

> **For literary and informational text:** Cite textual evidence to support analysis of what the text says explicitly as well as inferences drawn from the text.

Reading Standard 2:

For literary and informational text: Determine a theme or central idea of a text and how it is conveyed through particular details; provide a summary of the text distinct from personal opinions or judgments.

Reading Standard 3:

For literary text: Describe how a particular story's or drama's plot unfolds in a series of episodes as well as how the characters respond or change as the plot moves toward a resolution.

For informational text: Analyze in detail how a key individual, event, or idea is introduced, illustrated, and elaborated in a text (e.g., through examples or anecdotes).

Reading Standard 4:

For literary text: Determine the meaning of words and phrases as they are used in a text, including figurative and connotative meanings; analyze the impact of a specific word choice on meaning and tone.

For informational text: Determine the meaning of words and phrases as they are used in a text, including figurative, connotative, and technical meanings.

Reading Standard 5:

For literary text: Analyze how a particular sentence, chapter, scene, or stanza fits into the overall structure of a text and contributes to the development of the theme, setting, and plot.

For informational text: Analyze how a particular sentence, paragraph, chapter, or section fits into the overall structure of a text and contributes to the development of the ideas.

Reading Standard 6:

For literary text: Explain how an author develops the point of view of the narrator or speaker in a text.

For informational text: Determine the author's point of view or purpose in a text and explain how it is conveyed in the text.

Reading Standard 7:

For literary text: Compare and contrast the experience of reading a story, drama, or poem to listening to or viewing an audio, video, or live version of the text, including contrasting what they "see" and "hear" when reading the text to what they perceive when they listen or watch.

For informational text: Integrate information presented in different media or formats (e.g., visually, quantitatively) as well as in words to develop a coherent understanding of a topic or issue.

Reading Standard 8:

For literary text: (does not apply)

For informational text: Trace and evaluate the argument and specific claims in a text, distinguishing claims that are supported by reasons and evidence from claims that are not.

Reading Standard 9:

For literary text: Compare and contrast texts in different forms or genres (e.g., stories and poems; historical novels and fantasy stories) in terms of their approaches to similar themes and topics.

For informational text: Compare and contrast one author's presentation of events with that of another (e.g., a memoir written by and a biography on the same person).

Reading Standard 10:

For literary text: By the end of the year, read and comprehend literature, including stories, dramas, and poetry, in the grades 6–8 complexity band proficiently, with scaffolding as needed at the high end of the range.

For informational text: By the end of the year, read and comprehend literary nonfiction in the grades 6–8 text complexity band proficiently, with scaffolding as needed at the high end of the range.

Grade 7

Reading Standard 1:

For literary and informational text: Cite several pieces of textual evidence to support analysis of what the text says explicitly as well as inferences drawn from the text.

Reading Standard 2:

For literary text: Determine the theme or central idea of a text and analyze its development over the course of the text; provide an objective summary of the text.

For informational text: Determine two or more central ideas in a text and analyze their development over the course of the text; provide an objective summary of the text.

Reading Standard 3:

For literary text: Analyze how particular elements of a story or drama interact (e.g., how setting shapes the characters or plot).

For informational text: Analyze the interactions between individuals, events, and ideas in a text (e.g., how ideas influence individuals or events, or how individuals influence ideas or events).

Reading Standard 4:

> **For literary text:** Determine the meaning of words and phrases as they are used in a text, including figurative and connotative meanings; analyze the impact of rhymes and other repetitions of sounds (e.g., alliteration) on a specific verse or stanza of a poem or section of a story or drama.

> **For informational text:** Determine the meaning of words and phrases as they are used in a text, including figurative, connotative, and technical meanings; analyze the impact of a specific word choice on meaning and tone.

Reading Standard 5:

> **For literary text:** Analyze how a drama's or poem's form or structure (e.g., soliloquy, sonnet) contributes to its meaning.

> **For informational text:** Analyze the structure an author uses to organize a text, including how the major sections contribute to the whole and to the development of the ideas.

Reading Standard 6:

> **For literary text:** Analyze how an author develops and contrasts the points of view of different characters or narrators in a text.

> **For informational text:** Determine an author's point of view or purpose in a text and analyze how the author distinguishes his or her position from that of others.

Reading Standard 7:

> **For literary text:** Compare and contrast a written story, drama, or poem to its audio, filmed, staged, or multimedia version, analyzing the effects of techniques unique to each medium (e.g., lighting, sound, color, or camera focus and angles in a film).

> **For informational text:** Compare and contrast a text to an audio, video, or multimedia version of the text, analyzing each medium's portrayal of the subject (e.g., how the delivery of a speech affects the impact of the words).

Reading Standard 8:

> **For literary text:** (does not apply)

> **For informational text:** Trace and evaluate the argument and specific claims in a text, assessing whether the reasoning is sound and the evidence is relevant and sufficient to support the claims.

Reading Standard 9:

> **For literary text:** Compare and contrast a fictional portrayal of a time, place, or character and a historical account of the same period as a means of understanding how authors of fiction use or alter history.

For informational text: Analyze how two or more authors writing about the same topic shape their presentations of key information by emphasizing different evidence or advancing different interpretations of fact.

Reading Standard 10:

For literary text: By the end of the year, read and comprehend literature, including stories, dramas, and poetry, in the grades 6–8 complexity band proficiently, with scaffolding as needed at the high end of the range.

For informational text: By the end of the year, read and comprehend literary nonfiction in the grades 6–8 text complexity band proficiently, with scaffolding as needed at the high end of the range.

Grade 8

Reading Standard 1:

For literary and informational text: Cite the textual evidence that most strongly supports an analysis of what the text says explicitly as well as inferences drawn from the text.

Reading Standard 2:

For literary text: Determine a theme or central idea of a text and analyze its development over the course of the text, including its relationship to the characters, setting, and plot; provide an objective summary of the text.

For informational text: Determine a central idea of a text and analyze its development over the course of the text, including its relationship to supporting ideas; provide an objective summary of the text.

Reading Standard 3:

For literary text: Analyze how particular lines of dialogue or incidents in a story or drama propel the action, reveal aspects of a character, or provoke a decision.

For informational text: Analyze how a text makes connections among and distinctions between individuals, ideas, or events (e.g., through comparisons, analogies, or categories).

Reading Standard 4:

For literary and informational text: Determine the meaning of words and phrases as they are used in a text, including figurative, connotative, and technical meanings; analyze the impact of specific word choices on meaning and tone, including analogies or allusions to other texts.

Reading Standard 5:

For literary text: Compare and contrast the structure of two or more texts and analyze how the differing structure of each text contributes to its meaning and style.

For informational text: Analyze in detail the structure of a specific paragraph in a text, including the role of particular sentences in developing and refining a key concept.

Reading Standard 6:

For literary text: Analyze how differences in the points of view of the characters and the audience or reader (e.g., created through the use of dramatic irony) create such effects as suspense or humor.

For informational text: Determine an author's point of view or purpose in a text and analyze how the author acknowledges and responds to conflicting evidence or viewpoints.

Reading Standard 7:

For literary text: Analyze the extent to which a filmed or live production of a story or drama stays faithful to or departs from the text or script, evaluating the choices made by the director or actors.

For informational text: Evaluate the advantages and disadvantages of using different mediums (e.g., print or digital text, video, multimedia) to present a particular topic or idea.

Reading Standard 8:

For literary text: (does not apply)

For informational text: Delineate and evaluate the argument and specific claims in a text, assessing whether the reasoning is sound and the evidence is relevant and sufficient; recognize when irrelevant evidence is introduced.

Reading Standard 9:

For literary text: Analyze how a modern work of fiction draws on themes, patterns of events, or character types from myths, traditional stories, or religious works such as the Bible, including describing how the material is rendered now.

For informational text: Analyze a case in which two or more texts provide conflicting information on the same topic and identify where the texts disagree on matters of fact or interpretation.

Reading Standard 10:

For literary text: By the end of the year, read and comprehend literature, including stories, dramas, and poetry, in the grades 6–8 complexity band proficiently.

For informational text: By the end of the year, read and comprehend literary nonfiction at the high end of the 6–8 text complexity band independently and proficiently.

Appendix B

The Other Literacy Standards

(www.corestandards.org)

Here are the Anchor Standards for writing, speaking and listening, and language, thumbnailed by my own simplified wording of the standards.

The Writing Anchor Standards

Types and Purposes:

1. Write arguments: *Write arguments to support claims in an analysis of substantive topics or texts, using valid reasoning and relevant and sufficient evidence.*

2. Write informative/explanatory texts: *Write informative/explanatory texts to examine and convey complex ideas and information clearly and accurately through the effective selection, organization, and analysis of content.*

3. Write narratives: *Write narratives to develop real or imagined experiences or events using effective technique, well-chosen details, and well-structured event sequences.*

> **Note**
>
> In English language arts, teachers would be expected to address these three types of writing explicitly and individually, building the skills to be applied to the other subject areas. In the other subject areas, students may be expected to blend the three types into a single writing piece. For example, an anecdote or two strengthens argumentation, as does the inclusion of information (data, cause/effect statements, embedded definitions, explanations, etc.).

Production and Distribution:

4. Match your style to the expectations of the audience. *Produce clear and coherent writing in which the development, organization, and style are appropriate to task, purpose, and audience.*

5. Use the writing process: *Develop and strengthen writing as needed by planning, revising, editing, rewriting, or trying a new approach.*

6. Use technology as a collaborative tool: *Use technology, including the Internet, to produce and publish writing and to interact and collaborate with others.*

Research to Build and Present Knowledge:

7. Conduct short as well as more sustained research projects. *Conduct short as well as more sustained research projects based on focused questions, demonstrating understanding of the subject under investigation.*

8. Gather information from multiple sources. Judge the accuracy of your sources. Use proper citations. Avoid plagiarism. *Gather relevant information from multiple print and digital sources, assess the credibility and accuracy of each source, and integrate the information while avoiding plagiarism.*

9. Use both literary and informational texts to support, inform, and enrich your claims: *Draw evidence from literary or informational texts to support analysis, reflection, and research.*

Range of Writing:

10. Write routinely; write **both** formally and informally, depending on the expectations of the audience; write polished pieces, revised over time; **also,** write on-demand pieces within a short time frame, such as a single class period; use writing as **both** a means for learning and a way to demonstrate your knowledge: *Write routinely over extended time frames (time for research, reflection, and revision) and shorter time frames (a single setting or a day or two) for a range of tasks, purposes, and audiences.*

Regarding the range and content of the Writing Standards, the Core Standards document (www.corestandards.org) says this:

> For students, writing is a key means of asserting and defending claims, showing what they know about a subject, and conveying what they

have experienced, imagined, thought, and felt. To be college- and career-ready writers, students must take task, purpose, and audience into careful consideration, choosing words, information, structures, and formats deliberately. They need to know how to combine elements of different kinds of writing—for example, to use narrative strategies within argument and explanation within narrative—to produce complex and nuanced writing. They need to be able to use technology strategically when creating, refining, and collaborating on writing. They have to become adept at gathering information, evaluating sources, and citing material accurately, reporting findings from their research and analysis of sources in a clear and cogent manner. They must have the flexibility, concentration, and fluency to produce high-quality first-draft text under a tight deadline as well as the capacity to revisit and make improvements to a piece of writing over multiple drafts when circumstances encourage or require it. (p. 41)

The Speaking and Listening Anchor Standards

Comprehension and Collaboration:

1. **Develop socially acceptable conversation skills:** Prepare for and participate effectively in a range of conversations and collaborations with diverse partners, building on others' ideas and expressing their own clearly and persuasively.

2. **Verbally summarize information that you've heard or read:** Integrate and evaluate information presented in diverse media and formats, including visually, quantitatively, and orally.

3. **Assess the credibility of what you read and hear:** Evaluate a speaker's point of view, reasoning, and use of evidence and rhetoric.

Presentation of Knowledge and Ideas:

4. **Present meaningful ideas and information coherently and courteously:** Present information, findings, and supporting evidence such that listeners can follow the line of reasoning and the organization, development, and style are appropriate to task, purpose, and audience.

5. **Enhance formal presentations with visuals, including digital media:** Make strategic use of digital media and visual displays of data to express information and enhance understanding of presentations.

6. **Know the rules of formal spoken English and apply them when appropriate to the audience:** Adapt speech to a variety of contexts and communicative tasks, demonstrating command of formal English when indicated or appropriate.

Regarding the range and content of the Speaking and Listening Standards, the Core Standards document (www.corestandards.org) says this:

> To become college and career ready, students must have ample opportunities to take part in a variety of rich, structured conversations—as part of a whole class, in small groups, and with a partner—built around important content in various domains. They must be able to contribute appropriately to these conversations, to make comparisons and contrasts, and to analyze and synthesize a multitude of ideas in accordance with the standards of evidence appropriate to a particular discipline. Whatever their intended major or profession, high school graduates will depend heavily on their ability to listen attentively to others so that they are able to build on others' meritorious ideas while expressing their own clearly and persuasively.
>
> New technologies have broadened and expanded the role that speaking and listening play in acquiring and sharing knowledge and have tightened their link to other forms of communication. The Internet has accelerated the speed at which connections between speaking, listening, reading, and writing can be made, requiring that students be ready to use these modalities nearly simultaneously. Technology itself is changing quickly, creating a new urgency for students to be adaptable in response to change. (p. 48)

The Language Anchor Standards

The six Language Standards center around cultivating an academic and business-like tone over the years of a student's K–12 education. The Language Standards, especially the first three (which pertain to grammar), comprise the content of what English Language Arts teachers are expected to teach. As you can see, these Standards actually outline a much-needed scope and sequence for grammar instruction at grade levels 6–12. Standards 4 and 5 address vocabulary in a way that applies primarily to English Language Arts teachers. Standard 6 addresses vocabulary and language use (choices in how we express ourselves) that applies directly to all subjects. Really, all of the six Language Standards are folded into the other Standards that precede them.

Below are simplified statements of the Standards, followed by the original language (www.corestandards.org).

Conventions of Standard English

10. Know the rules of Standard written and spoken English and use them when your audience expects you to do so. Demonstrate command of the conventions of standard English grammar and usage when writing or speaking.

(Grade 6)

a. Ensure that pronouns are in the proper case (subjective, objective, possessive).

b. Use intensive pronouns (e.g., myself, ourselves).

c. Recognize and correct inappropriate shifts in pronoun number and person.

d. Recognize and correct vague pronouns (i.e., ones with unclear or ambiguous antecedents).

(Grade 7)

e. Explain the function of phrases and clauses in general and their function in specific sentences.

f. Choose among simple, compound, complex, and compound-complex sentences to signal differing relationships among ideas.

g. Place phrases and clauses within a sentence, recognizing and correcting misplaced and dangling modifiers.

(Grade 8)

h. Explain the function of verbals (gerunds, participles, infinities) in general and their function in particular sentences.

i. Form and use verbs in the indicative, imperative, interrogative, conditional, and subjunctive mood.

j. Recognize and correct inappropriate shifts in verb voice and mood.

(Grades 9–10)

k. Use parallel structure.

l. Use various types of phrases (noun, verb, adjectival, adverbial, participial, prepositional, absolute) to convey specific meanings and add variety and interest to writing or presentations.

(Grades 11–12)

m. Apply the understanding that usage is a matter of convention, can change over time, and is sometimes contested.

n. Resolve issues of complex or contested usage, consulting references (e.g., *Merriam Webster's Dictionary of English Usage, Garners, Modern American Usage*) as needed.

11. The above includes the visuals of writing: capitalization, punctuation, and spelling.

    (Grade 6)

    a. Use punctuation (commas, parentheses, dashes) to set off nonrestrictive/parenthetical elements.

    b. Spell correctly. (Note that this applies to all grade levels, so we will not be repeating it: just be aware that spelling is not a forgotten Standard as we travel up the grade levels.)

    (Grade 7)

    c. Use a comma to separate coordinate adjectives.

    (Grade 8)

    d. Use punctuation (comma, ellipsis, dash) to indicate a pause or break.

    e. Use an ellipsis to indicate an omission.

    (Grades 9–10)

    f. Use a semicolon (and perhaps a conjunctive adverb) to link two or more closely related independent clauses.

    g. Use a colon to introduce a list or quotation.

    (Grades 11–12)

    h. Observe the hyphenation conventions.

12. Knowledge of Language:

    Understand that language is a changeable social contract, subject to legitimate disagreement about diction and usage depending upon audience, purpose, and level of formality.

    (Grade 6)

    a. Vary sentence structure patterns for meaning, reader/listener interest, and style.

    b. Maintain consistency in style and tone.

    (Grade 7)

    c. Choose language that expresses ideas precisely and concisely, recognizing and eliminating wordiness and redundancy.

    (Grade 8)

    d. Use verbs in the active and passive voice and in the conditional and subjunctive mood to achieve particular effects (e.g., emphasizing the actor or the action; expressing uncertainty or describing a state contrary to fact).

(Grades 9–10)

    e. Write and edit work so that it conforms to the guidelines in a style manual (e.g., *MLA Handbook*, Turabian's *A Manual for Writers*) appropriate for the discipline and writing type.

(Grades 11–12)

    f. Vary syntax for effect, consulting references (e.g., Tufte's *Artful Sentences*) for guidance as needed; apply an understanding of syntax to the study of complex texts when reading.

13. Vocabulary Acquisition and Use:

Use context, word parts, dictionaries, and other reference tools to figure out the meaning of words and phrases. Determine or clarify the meaning of unknown and multiple-meaning words and phrases based on grade level reading and content.

(Grades 6–12)

    a. Use context (e.g., the overall meaning of a sentence or paragraph; a word's position or function in a sentence) as a clue to the meaning of a word or phrase.

    b. Use common, grade-appropriate Greek or Latin affixes and roots as clues to the meaning of a word (e.g., *audience, auditory, audible; belligerent, bellicose, rebel; precede, recede, secede; analyze, analysis, analytical; advocate, advocacy; conceive, conception, conceivable*).

    c. Consult general and specialized reference materials (e.g., dictionaries, glossaries, thesauruses), both print and digital, to find the pronunciation of a word or determine or clarify its precise meaning, its part of speech, or its etymology.

    d. Verify the preliminary determination of the meaning of a word or phrase (e.g., by checking the inferred meaning in context or in a dictionary).

14. Understand that words can have multiple meanings, connotations, and other subtleties. Demonstrate an understanding of figurative language, word relationships and nuances in word meanings.

(Grades 6–12)

    a. Interpret figures of speech (e.g., personification, allusions, verbal irony, puns, euphemisms, oxymoron, hyperbole, paradox) in context and analyze their role in the text.

    b. Use the relationship between particular words (e.g., *cause/effect, part/whole, item/category, synonym/antonym, analogy*) to better understand each of the words.

c. Distinguish among the connotations (associations) of words with similar denotations (definitions) (e.g., *stingy, scrimping, economical, unwasteful, thrifty, frugal, prudent, conservative*).

15. Understand and use an academic/business-like level of vocabulary and grammar. Acquire and use accurately general academic and domain-specific words and phrases, sufficient for reading, writing, speaking, and listening at the college and career readiness level; demonstrate independence in gathering vocabulary knowledge when considering a word or phrase important to comprehension or expression.

References

Babbit, Natalie. *Tuck Everlasting* (Farrar, Strauss, Giroux, 1975).

Beers, Kylene. *When Kids Can't Read: What Teachers Can Do* (Portsmouth, NH: Heinemann, 2003).

Berger, Melvin. *Discovering Mars: The Amazing Story of the Red Planet* (Scholastic, 1995).

Calkins, Lucy, Mary Ehrenworth, and Christopher Lehman. *Pathways to the Common Core.* (Portsmouth, NH: Heinemann, 2012).

"Coming to Terms with the Common Core Standards." www.ascd.org/publications/ newsletters/policy-priorities/vol16/issue4/full/Coming-to-Terms-with-Common-Core-Standards.aspx. Accessed March 30, 2013.

Common Core Coach for American Literature and Informational Texts, I (New York: *Triumph Learning,* 2014.)

Cooper, Susan. *The Dark is Rising* (New York: Margaret K. McElderry Books, 1973).

Curtis, Christopher Paul. *The Watsons Go to Birmingham—1963* (New York: Random House Children's Books, 1995).

Dahl, Roald. *Matilda* (New York: Puffin Books, first published in Great Britain by Jonathan Cape Ltd., 1988).

Erickson, John R. *Hank the Cowdog: Book 1* (Perryton, TX: Maverick Books, 1983).

Fitzgerald, F. Scott. *The Great Gatsby* (New York: Scribner's, 1925).

Geiss, Theodor (aka Dr. Seuss). *Horton Hatches the Egg* (New York: Random House, 1940).

George, Jean Craighead. *Julie of the Wolves* (New York: Harper, 1972).

Goodrich, Frances and Albert Hackett. *The Diary of Anne Frank* (New York: NY Dramatists Play Service, Inc., 1959).

Hawthorne, Nathaniel. *The Scarlet Letter* (Penguin Classics, 1850, 2002).

Henry, O. "The Ransom of Red Chief." www.classicshorts.com/stories/redchief.html. Accessed December 8, 2013.

Krashen, Stephen D. "The Case for Narrow Reading." *Language.* No. 5 (2004): 17–19.

Krashen, Stephen D. *Writing: Research Theory and Application* (Torrance, CA: Laredo, 1984).

Krashen, Stephen D. www.sdkrashen.com/content/articles/narrow.pdf (n.d.)

Lee, Harper. *To Kill a Mockingbird* (New York: Warner Books, 1960).

Maloch, Beth and Randy Bomer. "Teaching About and With Informational Texts: What Does Research Teach Us?" *Language Arts.* Vol. 90, No. 6 (July 2013), 441–450.

National Governors Association Center for Best Practices and Council of Chief State School Officers. Common Core State Standards (Literacy). (Washington, D.C.: National Governors Association Center for Best Practices, Council of Chief State School Officers, 2010).

Newman, Susan B. "Books Make a Difference: A Study of Access to Literacy." *Reading Research Quarterly.* No. 3 (1999), 286–331.

Papanis, Alexandros. "The Greek Influence on the English Language The Greek Thesaurus of English." http://alexandrospapanis.blogspot.com/2009_09_20_archive.html. Accessed January 19, 2014.

Smith, Frank. *Twelve Easy Ways to Make Learning to Read Hard and 1 Difficult Way to Make It Easy: Selected Papers and Some Afterthoughts. Essays into Literacy.* Edited by Arvind Gupta (Portsmouth, NH: Heinemann, 1984).

Steinbeck, John. *Travels with Charley: In Search of America* (New York: Penguin, 1997, 1962).

Tovani, Chris. *Do I Really Have to Teach Reading?* (Portland, ME: Stenhouse, 2004).

Twain, Mark. *The Adventures of Tom Sawyer* (Austin, TX: Holt, Rinehart and Winston, 1876, 1998).

White, E.B. *Charlotte's Web* (New York: Harper Collins, 1952).

Willingham, Daniel T. "The Usefulness of Brief Instruction in Reading Comprehension Strategies." *American Educator.* Winter 2006/2007, 39–45.

Zimmerman, Susan and Chryse Hutchins. *7 Keys to Comprehension: How to Help Your Kids Read It and Get It!* (New York: Three Rivers Press, 2003).

For Product Safety Concerns and Information please contact our
EU representative GPSR@taylorandfrancis.com Taylor & Francis
Verlag GmbH, Kaufingerstraße 24, 80331 München, Germany